This excellent book bridges between humanitarian relief and development, exa. how, churches can be agents of long-term change for justice and compassion by strengthening their local community systems and building resilience. The authors draw on their lived experiences through their respective faith-based organizations, World Evangelical Alliance and Food for the Hungry, to develop the concept and practice of "shared resilience," giving practical examples of how churches can work collaboratively with local communities. Grounded in the theology of integral mission, the book is both a guide for churches about community transformation and a guide for transformation within the church itself. Recognizing the potential of local faith communities as first responders and agents of social and behavioral change, governments and secular NGOs have shown increasing interest in leveraging their strengths and resources, often in utilitarian and instrumentalized ways. A healthy church – engaged and resilient itself – is also equipped as an effective partner for sustained positive change for the whole community, in ways that reject the instrumentalization of love. The book is inspiring, practical and timely on the topic of church and community transformation

Jean Duff, MPH
President,
Joint Learning Initiative for Faith and Local Communities

We have always believed that communities are the first responders to crises. However, when this intervention is guided and strengthened by Christian values, it becomes stronger and much more rooted in grounded beliefs. *Creating Shared Resilience* is a book of reality, addressing critical issues for communities in need and clearly showing the reality from different perspectives by presenting living and tangible interventions from around the globe. This book takes us beyond what we read in reports and documents to where we can touch the truth. It helps us see from a different and closer perspective. Along with proposing solutions and suggestions, it is a good reference for every humanitarian worker to use in the given context, recognizing the risk of a negative impact as well as building on the positive impact.

Rev Christo Greyling
Senior Director, Faith and External Engagement,
World Vision International

The omnipresence of media makes us aware of natural and human-made catastrophes like never before. Disasters capture our imagination, but we rarely stop to reflect on their causes or our collective response. In *Creating Shared Resilience* Boan and Ayers bring exceptional clarity to the central role of local faith communities in the midst of suffering. The authors point us to a first principle we often fail to remember, namely that "structures are vulnerable because *people* are vulnerable." It is the task of local faith communities to create those structures of resilience that will transform societies before, during, and after disasters. For Christians, the central task of bearing witness to God's *shalom* finds expression through the missiological task of building true, just and trustworthy communities where love of God is always coupled with love of neighbor (Mark 12:31) and even enemy (Matt 5:44).

George Kalantzis, PhD
Professor of Theology,
Wheaton College, Illinois, USA

Living in a context where climate change, poor governance, and conflicts are slowly defining the destiny of people living in poverty, I find the resilience model that this book is proposing very helpful to faith leaders who are working hard to build resilient communities. The authors have proposed a model known as "shared resilience," a model that integrates theoretical frameworks, evidence, and theology of resilience. The argument for a shared resilience resonates well with the African view which is entrenched in communal living. This book shows that change happens when communities work together to build collaborative relationships that seek to build community resilience.

Martin Kapenda
National Coordinator, Micah Zambia

A book that is as timely as it is necessary, David Boan and Josh Ayers present a well-supported and thoughtful look at how the Local Faith Community can meet the needs of a hurting world while continuing to retain their identity in Christ. By focusing on spiritual growth, in addition to physical and psychological well-being, Boan and Ayers present a holistic model of resilience that is unique and easily adaptable to the many and diverse needs of a broken world. *Creating Shared Resilience: The Role of the Church in a Hopeful*

Future is filled with concrete examples and clear guides for the practitioner. It is a must read for anyone who is called to minister in the front lines of disaster around the world.

Elizabeth List, PsyD
Associate Professor of Psychology,
Chair, Department of Psychology, Sociology, and Criminal Justice,
Northwest Nazarene University, Nampa, Idaho, USA

David Boan and Josh Ayers both have extensive on-the-ground experience in disaster risk reduction and response, which makes them well suited to tackle the topic of shared resilience. By the very worlds they span, they achieve their goal of bringing the often divergent worlds of theology, ecclesiology and humanitarian aid and development together. Yet they do this with a generous inclusivity. Rooted in their understanding of Christian-based local faith communities, they seek engagement with people of all faiths. Indeed this is the only path to shared resilience and one that they point out is pathed with mercy, compassion, collaboration and a strong sense that we are only truly resilient together. Importantly they focus on the centrality of connection with people over techniques and theories. Pointing to the unique role of the church they show the importance of remembering that God provides us with a common grace to build a society that reflects his kingdom. This enables local faith communities to build genuine relationships with groups outside of themselves for the purpose of creating a shared resilience, and ultimately, a glimpse of shalom. This is an important book that will help overcome the inertia often present in local communities when it comes to this important topic.

Andre Van Eymeren
Managing Director, Centre for Building Better Community
Author, *Building Communities of the Kingdom*

This book is a presentation and discussion on the models and various experiences in humanitarian development, especially on disaster where local faith communities and non-government organizations are engaged.

The faith community will have to be responsible and respectful of others as we engage in a servant leader manner in the community God has called us to serve. We can be part of the whole process of restoration and healing by sharing spaces with all other stakeholders in the community. May a continued conversation happen within the local faith communities who are involved in the serious calling of making life easy, especially for the needy and the marginalized.

I strongly recommend this book be read and discussed among development workers, especially those in disaster response programs. And may a continued cycle of learning and practice be a source of levelling up that results in sharing equal space with those in the community.

Junel Chavez
Area Manager,
Share an Opportunity Philippines, Inc.
National Chairman,
Department of Social Welfare and Development Area Based Standard Network

Creating Shared Resilience

Langham
GLOBAL LIBRARY

Creating Shared Resilience

The Role of the Church in a Hopeful Future

David M. Boan and Josh Ayers

© 2020 David M. Boan and Josh Ayers

Published 2020 by Langham Global Library
An imprint of Langham Publishing
www.langhampublishing.org

Langham Publishing and its imprints are a ministry of Langham Partnership

Langham Partnership
PO Box 296, Carlisle, Cumbria, CA3 9WZ, UK
www.langham.org

Published in partnership with Micah Global
Micah Global
PO Box 381, Carlisle, CA1 9FE, United Kingdom
www.micahglobal.org

ISBNs:
978-1-78368-791-6 Print
978-1-78368-829-6 ePub
978-1-78368-830-2 Mobi
978-1-78368-831-9 PDF

British Library Cataloguing-in-Publication Data
A catalogue record for this book is available from the British Library.

ISBN: 978-1-78368-791-6

Cover & Book Design: projectluz.com

Contents

Foreword

Poverty and vulnerability are not the same everywhere! Yet, everywhere there is an opportunity to make a difference. *Creating Shared Resilience: The Role of the Church in a Hopeful Future* is an invaluable resource that invites local faith communities (LFCs) to play a more intentional role in taking stands for justice and compassion through building cohesive and resilient communities.

Why local faith communities? Because faith matters! It is part of everyday life and can either be an important agent of change or a major hindrance to development. The world's major religions are each guided by their "religiously grounded conception of justice." The German philosopher Jurgen Habermas speaks of the "meaning-endowing" function of religion in the public sphere. Yet, to what extent are LFCs aware of, able, or ready to speak up *for the rights of all who are destitute. . . . defend the rights of the poor and needy* (Prov 31:8–9)?

The authors of this book, David Boan and Josh Ayers, are already involved through their respective faith-based organizations, World Evangelical Alliance (WEA) and Food for the Hungry (FH), in serving as the voice of the voiceless, addressing issues of poverty and vulnerability! I, too, inspired by verses such as Matthew 25:34–40 and Micah 6:8, am involved with the Lebanese Society for Educational and Social Development (LSESD), that seeks through a holistic integrated approach to empower the church and serve the community. In fact, WEA, FH, and LSESD approach such challenges from complementary angles – advocacy, addressing basic needs, engaging and empowering the local church to be the *church in the community.*

The opportunity to make a positive difference presents itself even in the most complex of situations, and sometimes when least expected! In fact, our journey at LSESD has taught us to look for the opportunity in every challenging circumstance. In Lebanon, it took the influx of over one million Syrian refugees to challenge and prompt a considerable number of local Christian communities to step up and realize their mission as being sent out, as Jesus was, to serve the world.

Initially reluctant to respond to the needs of a people group that is perceived by many Lebanese as the "enemy," partnering faith communities were challenged as biblical verses that call for *welcoming the stranger, loving the enemy*, and *loving your neighbor as yourself* suddenly came to life before their eyes. As one pastor shared, "God is using our work with Syrian refugees to teach us about him, and the first lesson is *forgiveness*."

It was quite a learning curve for our partner LFCs particularly as they wrestled with such biblical values as non-conditionality and non-discrimination. Yet, in adopting these values they preserved the dignity of the care-recipients who came from diverse religious and ethnic backgrounds, creating in many the desire to want to know more about "the God you worship."

As they engaged together, relationships of trust were built. And as one mother noted: "The help you are providing us is never just material. It is not so much what you give in terms of money, but what you give in terms of hope." Indeed so, for in countries of the Middle East, religion is very much part of people's coping mechanism that enables them to regain hope and persevere. Moreover, when a person or family is forced to flee and leave their home, they lose much more than their physical place of residence. They lose their extended family and their sense of community which are their safety net! Understanding this, LFCs become their new community, their new safety net.

The transformation took place for the caregivers as well as care-recipients. As caregivers, they had to revisit their understanding of Scripture and eventually grasp the full meaning of the gospel as *word* and *deed* before they could set out to address basic needs, and start church-based education centers for conflict where psycho-social support was integrated into the education programs. They did so in obedience, and with compassion.

The huge and complex needs led to the mapping out of other service providers and networks to maximize the benefit. The outcome was more needs being met, but also tremendous opportunities for the previously inward-focused LFCs to interact with others and seek potential synergies, and in the process reflect their values.

The volume of the crisis – with one in four people in Lebanon a Syrian refugee – necessitated engaging Syrians in serving their fellow Syrians. The impact was equally positive as, despite being refugees themselves, the volunteers developed a sense of ownership and responsibility towards their own people, and gained the skills needed to address such needs. These are skills which they will take with them wherever they go next.

Local faith communities all around the world can play active and effective roles in responding to situations of crisis. Yet the purpose of this book is to draw attention to an equally important role that LFCs can play: a preventive one, that invests in strengthening and building up the resilience of vulnerable communities "before the fact" and so reduce the risk of a crisis. And, in the event of a crisis, increased resilience reduces the impact of the damage done, and enables a quick and healthy return to normal life. It offers a glimpse of the theology of hope and shares models of resilience that involve various stakeholders – individuals, churches, and organizations. I strongly recommend it.

Alia Abboud
Chief Development Officer
Lebanese Society for Educational and Social Development (LSESD)

Preface by David M. Boan

Who would not want to be stronger in the face of life's greatest challenges? What better pursuit than to help a community and neighbors to more easily recover from a crisis or suffer less harm from the blows life delivers now and then? As a psychologist working internationally, I have been helped by my Majority World[1] friends and colleagues to move beyond my Western worldview and the focus on the individual to a more community-based view of the world. Resilience, it seems, is as much about the community we live in as it is about personal strength or upbringing. For some time, I have been curious as to how exactly communities become resilient and about the role played by local faith communities. How do some communities manage to work together, impart strength to their community members, and pull together in a crisis? As a Christian, I have been especially curious about the unique role of the church as well as the larger local faith community (LFC) in that process. That role is sometimes divisive, even destructive, but I have also witnessed people of different faiths at work in their communities in ways that made all members of the community stronger. How does that work?

I heard a comment about our situation here in the USA where an economic boom has benefited some people more than others. A common defense of the rise in the economy is to say a rising tide lifts all boats, to which someone replied, what about people who do not own boats? Is that the role of the LFC, to work in the community in a way that ensures everyone has a boat of some form? Is this the living out of God's plan, that just as God extends grace to reconcile all people to him, the LFC is to work in a way that reconciles all people to his community? Could resilience be the evidence of community reconciliation? Those are the questions that motivated us to write this book.

In addressing these and other questions, this book is organized into six chapters. Chapter 1 asks the question, what is resilience? It looks at the evidence for resilience, considers the various models, and proposes a comprehensive model of resilience.

Chapter 2 considers the theology of resilience with an emphasis on the ecclesiology of resilience (i.e. how resilience is a way to understand one part

---

1. Also known as the "global south" or "developing world."

of the work of the church). We explore the theological basis for resilience and the implications of this for the church.

Chapter 3 proposes a model we call "Shared Resilience" where the emphasis is on the community and relational pillars of resilience. We then describe, in chapter 4, how all of this may be applied to individuals, churches, and organizations. Given all that we have said, what then should we do?

In chapter 5, we discuss several case stories that illustrate the resilience concepts. We then end with a set of conclusions in chapter 6.

We should say something about our terminology. In discussing what to call the local house of worship, we considered "church" to be rather narrow and exclusive of those who refer to their faith community by other terms. We see our views on resilience as applying widely, and so we settled on the term "local faith community" or LFC. We use the term "community at large" to refer to the broader community, both faith and non-faith members who have community membership in common. We use the term "church" as a sub-set of the local faith community when we think our comments particularly apply to the Christian church. Since our own worldview is decidedly Christian, that view will still be apparent at times, but our intent is to be inclusive of all faiths.

We also discuss two other forms of organizations: community not-for-profit organizations and government agencies. We use "non-government organization" or NGO to refer to all forms of private organizations and "agency" to refer to government agencies.

Finally, I want to thank my wife Andrea for her patient support and encouragement. I am also fortunate to have had the participation of Josh Ayers as co-author with his questions, feedback, and written contributions.

Preface by Josh Ayers

Catastrophe has a smell. I'll never forget it and I hope that most of us never experience it. It overwhelmed me as I stepped down out of our small, borrowed airplane into the blazing noonday sun of Port-au-Prince. I'd just arrived, three days after the January 2010 earthquake, with Engineering Ministries International (EMI), to perform structural evaluations on some of Haiti's medical infrastructure. My technical training meant that I understood how design and building practices and the quality of building materials could affect the earthquake resistance of structures, but nothing could have prepared me for the scope and scale of the destruction I encountered. As each day passed, punctuated by the occasional aftershock, my focus narrowed from the destruction that reached deep into the countryside, to the neighborhoods, the city streets, the buildings, the homes, and finally the people, the individuals left behind. It was then, like emerging from the thick, technical fog of dust and rubble, that I realized the truth of disasters. There was something more; something lurking behind the physicality of the destruction. It was the "why." The structures were vulnerable because the *people* were vulnerable. The people were vulnerable for social, political, economic, human, and environmental reasons; reasons that extended far beyond building practices and materials, but that directly influenced them all the same.

In *Disasters by Design* (1999), sociologist Dennis Mileti "argues that all risks and losses – whether associated with so-called natural perils or technological ones – are the result of decisions that communities, societies, organizations, and political actors make, or fail to make."[1] Tierney, a sociologist describing the sociocultural ingredients that go into those decisions, says, "Societal values and ingrained practices, ideologies and worldviews, various forms of social cognition (as opposed to individual psychology), belief systems, collective memories, other types of social constructions, and ideas that become influential through forms of collective behavior such as fads and crazes all play a role in the social production of risk."[2] Suddenly, there seemed to be nothing "natural" about disasters at all. Disasters aren't inevitable. Risk is socially and politically

---

1. Tierney, *Social Roots*, 38–39.
2. Tierney, 46.

constructed. And, as such, it dawned on me that the church certainly had quite a lot to say about disaster risk reduction and resilience.

I further explored the role of the local church in reducing risk and increasing resilience to disasters, this time in the Ayeyarwady River Delta of Myanmar. Thanks to the generosity of Tearfund UK and the mentorship of Joel Hafvenstein, I spent several weeks in Myanmar discovering just how influential the local church can be in optimizing (or hindering) critical social capital for resilience to cyclones. In fact, in one of the villages that recovered fastest from Cyclone Nargis, the social cohesion between Buddhist and Christian households was so strong and the social capital they shared was so valuable that, just before the cyclone made landfall, one Buddhist said her Christian neighbor, "We will stay. If we eat, we eat together. If we starve, we starve together."

This book is the next step in the discussion on the role of the local church in disaster risk reduction and resilience. I hope it contributes to bringing together the sometimes isolated worlds of theology, ecclesiology, and humanitarian relief and development. To God be the glory.

Introduction

How is it that some individuals and communities seem to suffer less harm than others when faced with comparable crises or disasters, and seem to cope with these impacts better and recover from harm more quickly? Are there individually or communally held characteristics that explain how some are more resilient than others? Does the local faith community (LFC) play a role or contribute in some way to cultivating these characteristics? Over the past ten years, resilience has received much attention in relief and development, as researchers seek to identify the qualities of resilience in the hope of developing these qualities in others.

Our aim in this book is to show how LFCs can use the evidence and models supporting resilience to expand their understanding of the contribution they make to local communities.

> As Amartya Sen (1999) has noted, for many among the extremely poor in the developing world, regardless of specific religious tradition, religious faith is an extremely important facet of their identity. . . . In other words, adherence to religious practices can complement other intrinsically valued aspects of human flourishing, such as safety, health, knowledge, meaningful work and play, self-direction, culture and so on.[1]

When local churches fulfill their mission of serving as a window to God's kingdom, they are demonstrating the most important features of a resilient community, and impacting those around them in a way that creates a more resilient community.

Thus, resilience is not something new. It is neither a new program for the church nor something that a church adopts when it wants to do a social program. It is a characteristic of the church. The research on resilience helps expand our understanding of how it works and what it takes to become an agent of resilience (meaning, a person or group that facilitates resilience in others).

Further, because resilience is related to how a healthy local faith community functions, we believe that understanding and adopting resilient practices will

---

1. Haynes, *Religion and Development*, 55.

strengthen an LFC. In other words, the benefits of building resilience accrue to those who practice it as well as to those who are served by it.

Finally, we propose our own model that integrates the theoretical frameworks, evidence, and theology of resilience. It is not that we think the world needs more models of resilience, but since we are suggesting something new, we think it should have a name. Because our view emphasizes building collaborative relationships, demonstrating mercy, and acting compassionately, we call it "shared resilience." In effect, in any community, we are only resilient when we are resilient together.

Background

Interest in the topic of resilience has grown as the frequency and intensity of disasters has increased. This change in disaster frequency is due to a variety of factors, including the rise of hydrometeorological disasters linked to climate change and the fact that more people are drawn to disaster-prone areas. No one looks to put themselves in harm's way, but the most disaster-prone areas – such as coastal areas where people fish or low-lying, fertile areas with rich soil which are also prone to flooding – are often also areas of economic opportunity. EM-DAT, the International Disaster Database maintained by the Centre for Research on the Epidemiology of Disasters,[2] shows that the number of natural disasters reported every year has grown steadily, from an average of about 400 in the 1980s to 630 in the 1990s and to 730 in 2000s. (Note that while climate change cannot be linked to any single event, it is well established that climate change is the underlying cause of this trend.) As disasters increase, resilience has taken on greater importance as a possible way to reduce harm to individuals and communities. If greater resilience means less harm and quicker, more effective recovery, then, clearly, we should find ways to increase resilience. Further, the LFC, in its mission to care for those who are vulnerable and suffering, might find ways to strengthen that mission through an understanding of how to promote resilience. Indeed, the LFC may discover particular contributions to resilience that are unique to the LFC and consistent with its mission.[3] That, in a nutshell, is our aim in this book.

Linking resilience to disasters, however, presents challenges. One difficulty is that resilience is often defined by the end we seek rather than by the way

---

2. https://www.emdat.be/.

3. Deneulin and Bano, *Religion in Development*; Haynes, *Religion and Development*; Todd, *Fast Living*.

it operates within a community or individual. Resilience is sometimes seen as the ability to resist harm from, and to recover from, shocks and stresses. There are two problems with this understanding. First, it narrows how we understand resilience, and this limits our ability to see the many and varied forms resilience can take and the strategies we can adopt to increase it. We will show that current research is addressing this limitation and starting to show the diverse and everyday nature of resilience. Second, the focus on disasters poses a challenge when working with LFCs. Linking resilience to disasters causes some to see it as an issue for disaster agencies and governments rather than for faith communities: LFCs may help when disaster strikes, but it is not the mission of the LFC to combat disasters. In fact some LFC leaders argue, quite fairly, that focusing on disasters can harm the LFC by allowing disaster work to compete with or confuse the true identity of the LFC. We think this is an understandable concern, and it is one that we speak to directly in this book. LFCs should never become disaster agencies or NGOs. The work of the LFC can, however, be informed by, and benefit from, a broader understanding of resilience. As the LFC serves the community, one of the results of that service can be a community that is more resilient when faced with a disaster. More importantly, what better demonstration of the healthy influence of the LFC than to help create a healthy, resilient community?

Why should an LFC be interested in resilience?

Since the end of World War II, the global evangelical church has wrestled with the tension between seeking converts and seeking justice. Particularly in the West, with its emphasis on the individual over the community, the primary role of the LFC was seen as bringing people to the point of conversion. This emphasis on individualism within the church has its historical roots in Luther's arguments that placed greater emphasis on personal revelation – "the priesthood of all believers." Naturally, the "brand" of Christianity that Western missionaries then brought to the Majority World reflected the culture from which they came. This holds true for relief and development "evangelists" as well, underplaying the role of social capital in resilience, preferring terms like "self-sustaining" or "self-reliance," while disdaining ideas of "interdependence" or dependence of any kind. The Enlightenment and the Second Awakening also had profound influences on the understanding of the communal nature of God's kingdom. God as the source for human value and dignity was replaced by humanity itself. Saint Augustine, and later Martin Luther, described this as *incurvatus in se*, or being curved inward on oneself. The communal effort of seeking after the mutually beneficial kingdom was replaced by a society of individuality, human reason and achievement. Individual wealth and prestige, driven by the insatiable thirst for efficiency, became the benchmark of human progress.

This emphasis on the individual was a poor model for the Majority World and its more communally focused cultures. The Lausanne Covenant of 1974 addressed this over-emphasis on individualism by saying that "evangelism and sociopolitical action are both part of our Christian responsibility."[4] The issue, however, was far from settled. While faith-based organizations embraced this as evangelism through development, many voiced concerns about the "social gospel" and the dilution of evangelism through social works. Furthermore, some argue that the increasing involvement of faith-based organizations and civil society organizations in community development further encourages the LFC to abdicate its social responsibilities.

This tension exists even while efforts to reconcile evangelism with social responsibility continue. Some suggest that we view conversion as an end point, with ministering to the community seen as part of the process. Others point to the parable of the good Samaritan or Jesus's admonition to "love your neighbor as yourself" and call for those examples to be embedded into our Christian walk. This book offers another view in this ongoing discussion.

While we focus on understanding resilience and the LFC's role in creating resilient communities, we acknowledge the concern among some groups that when LFCs engage in social ministry, they risk becoming indistinguishable from social service agencies. If that happens, then what becomes of their witness? How are they a light to God's kingdom if their light is seen as something any secular agency can do? Our response to this concern is to acknowledge it as real and then show how the LFC can be socially active in ways that are unique to the LFC while upholding standards of quality and effectiveness. The Christian community in particular has a unique identity as the redeemed and reconciled "body" of diverse disciples of Christ, endowed with "different kinds of gifts, but the same Spirit . . . different kinds of service, but the same Lord . . . different kinds of working, but the same God" (1 Cor 12:4–6 paraphrased). The Christian church does not *become* the body of Christ *because* it behaves a certain way. It simply *is,* as a result of its faith in Christ's love and redeeming power on the cross. When the Christian church exercises its unique capabilities, it is evincing its unique identity to the glory of God. In the same way, expressing these unique capabilities for the benefit of people and

---

4. https://www.lausanne.org/content/covenant/lausanne-covenant.

whole communities is an expression of faith that distinguishes the Christian church from other community actors. Thus, evangelism is not the only way for the church to serve others, and social service need not be a threat to the witness of the church.

We also see that there is a growing interest by governments and NGOs in greater collaboration with LFCs as partners in development. This trend began in the 1990s, culminating most recently and publicly with the 2016 Special Session on Religious Engagement at the World Humanitarian Summit in Istanbul. A United Nations Inter-Agency Task Force on Engaging Faith-Based Actors for Sustainable Development emphasized the inclusion of faith-based actors in their Sustainable Development Goals (SDGs). The Task Force noted many contributions from LFCs, including the following:

- Because LFCs are the community at large, they can respond quickly to a variety of challenges, including preventing conflict, responding to a disaster, and advocating for those in need.
- They play a core role in local response mechanisms.
- They can mobilize local support for peace and stability.[5]

The attention on LFCs is growing as governments and international non-government organizations (INGOs) seek to leverage the strengths and resources of LFCs. This, however, has not always been good news for LFCs.

> Despite the contribution of faith and LFCs, they appear marginalised for two reasons. Firstly, they are local in an internationally dominated sector and, secondly, they are faith-based in a secularised system. Furthermore, there are widespread misconceptions concerning the role of faith groups in this area. Where partnerships do occur, there is a risk of faith groups being "instrumentalised," that is, used as channels of assistance with little regard to their own motivations and assets.[6]

This utilitarian view of LFCs by some governments and some NGOs shapes their approach to working with LFCs as they seek to enhance their own access to the community at large, capitalize on the expertise of local culture, borrow acceptance and credibility, and more. The growing attention to LFCs only serves to highlight the view of many that the LFC, when engaged in this way, is indistinguishable from secular actors. What does the LFC offer, in terms of

---

5. Joint Learning Initiative on Faith & Local Communities, "Evidence for Religious Groups' Contributions," 1–2.

6. Fiddian-Qasmiyeh and Ager, "Local Faith Communities," 9.

community development, that any secular civil society organization cannot offer?

The current LFC/INGO partnership model is not a simple relationship either for those who would engage LFCs or for the LFCs themselves. For example, Burchardt[7] notes how partnerships between LFCs and the government to reduce the spread of HIV/AIDS in South Africa fundamentally changed the mission of many of the participating LFCs. Other authors have noted that LFCs should learn to be more like INGOs so that they would be more effective partners and co-implementers. Some (including the authors) see this as both a corruptive influence and a failure to recognize the unique and essential relationship between the LFC and the wider community. Other authors note that unintended consequences are present whenever a strong, well-resourced, or influential entity partners with those who have less power or resources. Sometimes, this may come about when the less powerful mimic those with more power. Other times, it may be as a result of direct coercion. Compounding the problem is the fact that these disparate power relationships most often occur with LFCs serving poor communities. When an LFC struggles to survive with support from just the local community, the temptation to attract resources by partnering with an INGO or government is very powerful. In such cases, it is easy to justify crafting the LFC mission to attract outside support.

Some LFCs are very aware of this issue, and they struggle with it. Boan et al. found that in the Philippines, pastors were split over whether or not they should work with the government. One group saw it as enabling a larger mission; others described it as a pact with the devil that would undermine the church.[8]

Whatever the cause of the problem, helping the LFC to see that it has resources, influence, and roles separate from outside entities can reduce this risk. An LFC with a clear sense of the role it plays in the community and the valuable contributions it can make to a partnership is less likely to succumb to the temptation to emulate a wealthier partner. This emphasizes the importance of clarifying the LFC's cultural mandate, namely that God calls us to be agents not only of his saving grace, but also of his common grace. Our job is not only to build up the LFC but also to build a society to the glory of God. Colson and Pearcey put it this way:

> As agents of God's common grace, we are called to help sustain and renew his creation, to uphold the created institutions of family

---

7. Burchardt, "Faith-Based Humanitarianism," 30–55.
8. Boan et al., "Disasters, Social Justice."

and society, to pursue science and scholarship, to create works of art and beauty, and to heal and help those suffering from the results of the Fall.[9]

Taking up the LFC's role in building community resilience would be a significant contribution to this end. It would help make LFCs more powerful partners in development and provide guidance on the safest and most effective approaches to engage in the community.

Not only do we suggest looking differently at the role of the LFC, we also suggest a different view of disasters, whether natural or human-made. The evidence showing the disparate social consequences of disasters is growing. Just this month a US government report revealed that government disaster aid is disproportionately distributed, with the majority class and the wealthier receiving more and the poor and minorities receiving significantly less assistance. This is consistent with evidence showing that following a natural disaster the upper economic classes and the better educated tend to become wealthier, while the poor and less educated suffer a decline in wealth.[10] Increasing frequency and severity of disasters is one of the drivers of economic inequality.[11] This suggests a close link between disaster impacts and social issues of disparity, inequity, and injustice. We see this as a compelling argument for the necessity to have LFCs participate in creating resilience.

In communities in northeastern Congo, an area that has seen over thirty years of violence, local faith leaders have become the main source of support for villagers. Although the faith leaders have suffered as much as the rest of the community, they respond with compassion while also working to engage their congregations in becoming sources of care and protection. Likewise, in Ukraine, area faith leaders are organizing support caravans and providing food, firewood (in the winter), and medicine, combined with compassion and prayer. In an inner-city LFC in Minneapolis, members work to bring different cultures together, promoting understanding and finding ways to minister together. In Lebanon, LFCs are working tirelessly to respond to the needs of Syrian refugees in their midst, going beyond basic service provision to build the resilience necessary to cope with the long-term challenges of displacement. In communities of the Ayeyarwady River Delta of Myanmar, LFC leaders wisely and prophetically encouraged members to reach out to their Buddhist

---

9. Colson and Pearcey, *How Now Shall We Live?*, xii.

10. Elliott and Howell, "Beyond Disasters."

11. Howell and Elliott, "As Disaster Costs Rise," 1–2.

neighbors, helping to build deep social connections and social cohesion that would eventually prove critical for the resilience needed for those communities to cope with and recover from Cyclone Nargis. In other parts of the world, faith communities organize to support those who are marginalized and overlooked, advocating alongside them, giving voice to the voiceless. The Anglican Diocese of North Eastern Caribbean and Aruba created a youth telephone hotline to support youth and adolescents with accurate information on HIV/AIDS and other issues and to provide a confidential network referral service to social service organizations. In the Philippines, the National Council of Churches in the Philippines created the Child-Friendly Local Church Communities (CFLCC) initiative which published Bible-based guides on children's rights.

The question we consider here is how these acts of ministry and service, and even the more transcendental, intangible investments in the spiritual growth of its members, impact the people and culture of their broader community. Are they sources of exclusively individual impact or is there a broader sociocultural impact? If there is a sociocultural impact, what is the nature of that impact, is it beneficial for the community, and should we seek to increase it? For the LFC, how do we understand this impact and its connection to the ministry of the LFC? Is there a theology of community engagement and resilience?

In this book, we consider the concept of resilience as a lens through which we might learn how the LFC – referring to the local Christian house of worship and other houses of worship and the broader networks to which they belong – contributes to healthier, stronger communities. We are not examining *resilience* so much as using it as a framework through which we look at how an LFC contributes to the strength of a community. In doing this, we start with an example that illustrates what we want to understand about LFCs and communities. We then provide an overview of the current models for resilience in communities, with an eye specifically toward the role of the LFC in the community and how or when that role adds to (or in some cases detracts from) resilience. We look at the social sciences and specify a set of characteristics that are associated with resilience. We then consider the theological support for applying these models to the LFC and give an overview of the debate over the proper role of the LFC and the rise of integral mission. Finally, we propose a set of recommendations or guidelines for the role of the LFC in building and maintaining resilience within the community.

1

What Is Resilience?

Personal and community resilience is a metaphor drawn from physical science.[1] In physics, a material is resilient when it can absorb energy and be deformed, and then release that energy and return to its original state. The materials metaphor is evident in the United Nations Office for Disaster Risk Reduction (UNDRR) terminology, which defines "resilience" as

> the ability of a system, community or society exposed to hazards to resist, absorb, accommodate, adapt to, transform and recover from the effects of a hazard in a timely and efficient manner, including through the preservation and restoration of its essential basic structures and functions through risk management.[2]

In other words, resilience is the capacity of just about anything to return to its original, pre-stressed state after exposure to external forces. Metaphorically, practitioners and academics often compare resilience to the "elasticity" of a rubber band. If the rubber band can adequately "absorb" the stress from an external force without losing its integrity or changing its internal properties, it can return to its original condition without long-term harm. While the metaphor applies to a system's absorptive capacity, it is unable to account for other resilience capacities such as the ability to adapt to recurrent shocks and stresses or to transform altogether.

While the notion of resilience has been used for centuries by scholars and non-specialists alike, it is only recently that the humanitarian relief and development sector has adopted this metaphor to illustrate the ability of a person, household, community, or system to recover from shocks and stresses. A search in academic journals published between 1960 and 2018 for the words

---

1. Holling, "Resilience and Stability."
2. https://www.unisdr.org/we/inform/terminology.

"resilience," "disaster," and "development" showed a nearly 1700-fold increase, demonstrating the increase in usage of resilience by relief and development practitioners and academics.

What is behind this growing fascination with resilience in relief and development discourse? Some appreciate the "semantic ability [of resilience] to represent a readily recognizable concept."[3] Resilience provides a familiar taxonomy for many from diverse backgrounds to immediately get a sense of the same notion.[4] Indeed, Béné et al. claim that the "relatively loose meaning of resilience . . . creates communication bridges and platforms between disciplines and communities of practice" which ordinarily would not collaborate.[5]

Resilience also helps to "train the spotlight once again on human agency as the main vehicle for change" socioeconomically.[6] Particularly when dealing with covariate shocks or stresses, or those "simultaneously affecting groups of households or even entire communities (Heltberg 2007)"[7], the ways in which socially connected stakeholders share vulnerabilities and capacities is critical.

Adopting a resilience approach or perspective can lead to investigating more purposefully the linkages between humanitarian and development action.[8] If we take the shock or stress event as a starting point, then we can build the ability to successfully absorb and recover from impacts before the event through disaster risk reduction. Resilience develops from preventing, mitigating, and preparing for the impacts as well as working with the local community to further develop positive coping strategies and mechanisms. Relief workers provide help during and immediately following the event in ways that prompt, promote, and facilitate more sustainable long-term recovery.

For millennia, LFCs have promoted and exhibited resilience without necessarily using the language of "resilience" as utilized by the secular relief and development industry. Meanwhile, the reverse is also true: LFCs use a religious vernacular not typically heard within relief and development circles. Fiddian-Qasmiyeh also cites Holton's work in southern Sudan:

> Working with the Dinka of Sudan, [Holton] cites an elder's account of his community's survival that is expressed in typical religious language: "Our hope comes from God. He is the air that

---

3. Bahadur et al., "The Resilience Renaissance?," 4.

4. Norris et al., "Community Resilience"; Béné et al., "Resilience: New Utopia?"

5. Béné et al., 12.

6. Weijer, "Resilience: A Trojan Horse?," iv.

7. Béné et al., "Resilience: New Utopia?," 11–12.

8. IFRC, "Road to Resilience."

we breathe. He is the sand that we walk on. Without him, we would not have made it, but through him, we will have a future."[9]

While expressing core tenets of his faith, this elder is nonetheless describing the inner source of his community's resilience and future hope. Elena Fiddian-Qasmiyeh and Alastair Ager go on to argue for more "bilingual" capacities from both sides of the religious-secular divide in order to improve everything from service provision and development outcomes to research. This book is, in part, an attempt to begin that journey of learning to speak these two dialects of the same language.

However, not everyone supports the popularity of the resilience model. To some, resilience is "inappropriate, imprecise, or 'glittery.'"[10] Others argue that "a simple and unreflecting application of the resilience concept into social and political matters will inevitably run into substantial difficulties."[11] Furthermore, some authors suggest that the use of the resilience metaphor is unfortunate as it narrows the focus to the response to a disruptive event as described from a materials perspective. The materials metaphor puts limits on how people think about and apply the concept of resilience.

A problem that can occur with any model is thinking that the model by itself is a complete solution to the problem; in this case, thinking that all we need to know about disaster risk is how to make people more resilient. It can lead people to think that the model is a full description of the phenomenon and cause us to overlook or fail to see alternative or expanded features (such as the social justice aspects of risk). As the statistician George Box said:

> Since all models are wrong, a scientist cannot obtain a "correct" one by excessive elaboration. On the contrary, following William of Occam, he should seek an economical description of natural phenomena. Just as the ability to devise simple but evocative models is the signature of the great scientist, so over-elaboration and overparameterization is often the mark of mediocrity.[12]

Capacities that reduce disaster risk and promote recovery are just one part of a well-functioning community. This is one of the criticisms aimed at the concept of resilience, namely that it focuses on adversity and ignores

---

9. Fiddian-Qasmiyeh and Ager, "Local Faith Communities," 17.
10. Norris et al., "Community Resilience," 128.
11. Béné et al., "Resilience: New Utopia?," 14.
12. Box, Hunter, and Hunter, *Statistics for Experimenters*, 440.

everyday aspects of resilience.[13] We see this as a problem of the attention given to major disasters rather than a problem with the resilience concept itself. There are everyday disruptive events that, like major disaster events, require resilience, but the former never make the news. The landmark Chronic Poverty Report issued by the Overseas Development Institute (ODI) in 2014 argued that household level shocks or stresses like the death of a productive family member, expenses associated a chronic illness, or dowries paid at weddings can often be enough to impoverish a household, erasing gains in income and well-being, sending it back below the poverty line once again.[14] Although these events do not rise to the level of community crisis, the same approaches as resilience in the face of disaster can be usefully employed to ensure more sustainable poverty escapes. Therefore, we consider a range of models of resilience and what in those models helps in understanding the role of the LFC. For example, Norris et al. suggest the term "population wellness for resilience," which they define as mental and physical health, role functioning, and quality of life across all community constituents.[15] They suggest that this incorporates the conventional view of resilience but distinguishes it from disaster response resources. These and other models show that the concept is evolving and moving away from a purely disaster focus. We propose that many of these various views of resilience have overlapping elements, and understanding these elements will help us understand the role of LFCs.

Thus, in our exploration of the LFC and resilience, we are not only concerned with how an LFC enhances individual resilience to, or preparation for, a disaster. We see the issue of individual versus communal views of resilience as two parts of a whole. People live within social and political contexts of a community, whose own systems and context are informed by dynamics happening at higher, broader scales. When the community has characteristics that foster individual resilience this benefits both the community and individuals. When many individuals in a community demonstrate resilience – particularly social and political forms of resilience – then the resilience of the community as a whole is greater.[16] Thus, we view resilience as a reciprocal process between the individual and the community. The emphasis on this reciprocal process is a contemporary view of resilience. The prior emphasis on individual resilience has given way to a contextualized view that asserts

13. Kirmayer et al., "Community Resilience."
14. Shepherd et al., *Chronic Poverty Report.*
15. Norris et al., "Community Resilience," 133.
16. Pelling, *Vulnerability of Cities.*

that social, political, and even natural environments matter more than was previously understood. A contextualized view looks at the environment and culture and how the individual interacts with them. In keeping with this, our focus is on how communities develop capacities for protection, support, and wellness of individuals that, in turn, strengthen the individual's development. In other words, our question is: What role does the LFC play in community characteristics that enhance the development of all members of that community and result in a more resilient community?

Fiddian-Qasmiyeh and Ager state, "DRR [disaster risk reduction] scholar Ben Wisner suggests that at present 'there is less activity by faith communities . . . in the areas of preparedness and prevention than in disaster response and recovery.'"[17] A contextualized view helps to correct this imbalance as it distinguishes between interactions and resources in a community that enhance community and individual functioning and those same capacities when the community or individual face a crisis. The contextualized view means not only focusing on disaster response to identify resilience but also considering the ongoing process of development that leads to a resilient response to a crisis. This is important because focusing on a crisis or disaster raises questions about the role of the LFC during a crisis. We answer that question by saying that community engagement by the LFC leads to healthy development and resilience when the LFC functions as God intended. Responding to crisis or disaster is not a special case of LFC functioning. Rather, it is a continuation of the ongoing role of the church in the community.

Another reason for not focusing solely on disasters is that resilience is part of everyday life, and not just important during a crisis. Ögtem-Young presents evidence that resilience is built up through everyday experiences.[18] While extreme events can reveal the state of individual and community resilience, it is through our response to everyday stressful events that we become more or less resilient. Further, just as faith is key to how we live our lives, it is also key to how we manage everyday events, and thus plays an important role in the development of resilience. While a disaster is something that overwhelms local capacity, there are also everyday disruptors that are personal crises even though they do not constitute a community "disaster." Community-level shocks or stresses like crime, conflict, or even social upheaval in the form of newly-arriving migrants can sometimes be enough to impoverish vulnerable households. While some may debate the LFC's role in disaster response, few

---

17. Fiddian-Qasmiyeh and Ager, "Local Faith Communities," 22.
18. Ögtem-Young, "Faith Resilience," 10.

would argue that the LFC has an important role in how we manage the everyday events and challenges in our lives.

Thus, we are saying that resilience has multiple dimensions, including important dimensions of faith, spirituality, and community. Resilience is neither fixed nor static, but an ongoing process of engaging with stressful events of widely varying intensities, determining what those events mean, and incorporating them into our life experience.

Is Resilience Relevant to the Mission of a Local Faith Community?

From the discussion above, it should be clear that just as there are many dimensions to resilience, there are many resilience-related dimensions to the role the LFC plays in the community.

To start with, we suggest that faith is not simply an *element* of resilience. Faith, when understood broadly, is *central* to resilience insofar as it shapes our worldview. In order to think, know, act, and make plans or prepare for the future, we use our experiences to construct a model of the world and then use this model as a reference. This worldview is developed socially through conversations, shared experiences, norms, and even education, including interactions in our LFC. All of these influence our view of what the world is like and how it operates. We must have faith that our model is a reliable guide to the world. Using our model is, in some respects, an act of faith. Our model includes an *epistemology* (i.e. beliefs about the nature and sources of knowledge), a *cosmology* (i.e. beliefs about the origins and nature of the universe, life, and especially man), a *teleology* (i.e. beliefs about the meaning and purpose of the universe, its inanimate elements, and its inhabitants), an *anthropology* (i.e. beliefs about the nature and purpose of man in general and oneself in particular), and an *axiology* (i.e. beliefs about the nature of value, what is good and bad, what is right and wrong).

In this broad sense, *all* people live by faith, though that faith may or may not have a *theological* element to it. This worldview tells us who and what are trustworthy, how to respond to challenging events, and how to solve problems. We can say that this model of the world and relationships directly impacts our resilience. Our relationships with God and the LFC, and with the people who represent God and the LFC, are critical factors determining our model of how the world works. In that sense, our faith and our spiritual relationships are one of the most basic determinants of our resilience.

Just as faith and spirituality can be positive elements of our resilience, they also have the potential to be negative. If our faith contains aspects of fear, negative emotions, isolation, and distrust, this can reduce resilience. Later, we will explain how this occurs, but our point here is that these negative coping strategies and mechanisms are yet another reason for understanding the connection between faith and resilience. Just as we want to promote and enhance the positive, we want to recognize and avoid negative contributors.

The idea of resilience is a key component of the trend mentioned in the introduction, where governments and INGOs (International Non-Governmental Organization) desire to engage LFCs in development and humanitarian action. The narrow and technical definition of resilience suggests it is the domain of technical actors from whom LFCs need to learn, rather than a way of understanding how LFCs may already operate in the community. Some experts have spoken out against this as the institutionalization of compassion.[19] This is a fundamental misunderstanding of the relationship between LFCs and communities. LFCs have engaged in community building and community health for two millennia.[20] Suggesting that they need to be engaged by governments or INGOs in order to more effectively serve communities is at best, flawed, and at worst, patronizing and arrogant. We will argue that it is important for LFCs to have a foundational understanding of resilience as defined by the technical relief and development community and to be able to relate that understanding to the role of the LFC, and indeed to the congruences of the LFC's historical activities and those of the relief and development community. This understanding will, ideally, help LFCs advocate for their rightful place in community development and speak the technocratic language of relief and development partners. In particularly poor and vulnerable communities, domestic and international development agencies – including governments – will almost certainly be active, initiating new relief and development projects regularly, often without the consent of the LFC and in ways that leave the LFC powerless to influence. In a sense, the secular relief and development game is one that LFCs will increasingly find themselves forced to play. If the LFC has its community's best interests in mind, to withdraw and withhold is not an effective strategy. Fiddian-Qasmiyeh and Ager, researchers studying the role of LFCs in building community resilience, express it clearly:

---

19. Samuel, "Doing Justice."

20. For a further discussion of this role, see the WEA brief to the UN on the role of evangelical communities in development, available at http://www.worldea.org/news/4585/wea-submits-brief-on-the-evangelical-community-and-humanitarian-development-to-united-nations-world-humanitarian-summit.

They [LFCs] are inadequately represented at the planning and coordination table, and their scalability remains unexplored. As a result, development and humanitarian actors do not always understand their motivations and contributions.[21]

LFC's need not allow the work of community resilience to be defined away as a technical activity outside of the normal functioning of the LFC. Understanding resilience in broader terms that are more relevant to the faith community can position LFCs to see their unique role and contribution and resist allowing governments and INGOs to define it away from the normal and traditional practices of LFCs.

It is also important that LFCs understand resilience apart from secular partnerships. Many authors suggest that the evangelical community has a strong framework for personal evangelism and a vague framework for community engagement. Having a poorly understood theological framework for community engagement limits the LFC's effectiveness and may even be a community risk factor. Understanding resilience can provide language for the actions of LFCs that have community impact, and thus expand the way certain actions and their consequences – both positive and negative – are understood. This can allow LFCs to be more deliberate in their ministries and to more fully engage people who want to see that their ministry has an impact.

Finally, resilience is a contemporary way of understanding the historical and unique role of the LFC. An important part of the value to LFCs of understanding resilience is that it positions them to be full partners in development, especially when partnering with secular actors. The role of LFCs in community resilience can include actions that are expressions of the nature of LFCs and which cannot be replicated by secular actors. Thus, when properly understood by both LFCs and secular actors, the LFC's role becomes essential to a whole community approach to development. This makes LFCs powerful agents for change, not the passive supporters of external policies that they sometimes become.

Evidence for the Relationship between LFCs and Community Resilience

Faith today is treated as something that only should make us different, not that actually does or can make us different. In reality,

---

21. Fiddian-Qasmiyeh and Ager, "Local Faith Communities," 9.

we vainly struggle against the evils of this world, waiting to die
and go to heaven. Somehow we've gotten the idea that the essence
of faith is entirely a mental and inward thing.[22]

The evidence for the diverse and impactful relationship between the LFC
and the community is growing. One area of study is the role of the LFC in
disasters. Cheema et al. describe the complex relationship between LFCs that
have social, political, cultural, and economic dimensions.[23] Studying the ways
LFCs helped community members recover from a disaster, they describe a
diverse and multifaceted relationship between the LFC and the community. The
LFC initiatives included spiritual support, social reintegration, coordination
of relief, providing an access point for people in need of aid, and community
engagement. These diverse means of community engagement are often
overlooked and not well understood by governments and NGOs, thus limiting
the potential for more effective partnerships. For example, the authors describe
the role of the mosques following a major earthquake in Pakistan:

Taken as a whole, the institution of the mosque played distinctive
and multifaceted roles in post-disaster Pakistan. Socially and
culturally, the mosque served as an entry door, a bridge between
actors and across cultural differences, and facilitated access
to communities by private organisations, government, and
local, national and international NGOs during the earthquake
response and relief. Unlike schools, hospitals, and government
organisations, which stopped functioning due to the destruction
of their infrastructure, the institution of the mosque proved to be
indestructible. The mosque functioned well beyond the limits of
men and material, brick and mortar. The mosque building may
have been destroyed, but the institution of the mosque remained
functional and effective. It continued to serve its surviving
community.[24]

Clark looked at the role of local Christian communities in community
development in Vanuatu.[25] In addition to describing programs for youth,
women, and the poor, and health, education, and advocacy services, he makes
two interesting observations. One is the creation of space for programming not

---

22. Dallas Willard, cited by Stearns, *Hole in Our Gospel.*
23. Cheema et al., "Unnoticed but Important."
24. Cheema et al., 2221.
25. Clarke, "Good Works."

otherwise available in the community. LFCs used their facilities as a program resource. He also notes the lack of distinction between the spiritual ministry and community programs. The work of the LFC became increasingly holistic, with community programs being part of reaching people spiritually.

> Within Vanuatu, Christian churches play a central role in the provision of social services in both urban and rural locations. Since the earliest missionaries, there has been a convergence of devotional and non-devotional activities organized, implemented, and located within the churches. Even after more than 100 years of active Ni-Vanuatu mission, the needs of rural communities continue to exist and therefore must be met. "We are in the world, and these are challenges that we face" (Interviewee C10). While the ordained Christian leaders have not necessarily led these activities, they have been clearly articulated and understood as church ministry activities.[26]

Models of Resilience

There are several ways in which resilience is described in the research literature and among practitioners. We will review several of these models and consider their relevance for the LFC as we work toward a model of the LFC and community resilience.

Resilience and the Trustworthy Community

Rolf Lidskog describes a revealing connection between how a community views their experience of an extreme event and the subsequent resilience of that community.[27] Lidskog suggests that the impact of an extreme event connects to how the community evaluates the event – that is, what they think it reveals about the nature of the community. The emotional impact of a crisis is an important part of understanding how individuals are affected. Lidskog takes this view two steps further. He suggests that this evaluation occurs at the community level as well as the individual level. The evaluation of a disaster by the community impacts social cohesion and, by extension, the capacity for collaboration and joint caretaking. That sets the stage for the second part of

---

26. Clarke, 348.
27. Lidskog, "Invented Communities."

his view – that the community evaluation of an event impacts future resilience to a disaster.

Lidskog looked at communities that experienced the largest fire disaster ever to occur in Sweden. In considering these events and their impact, he notes that while the event (in this case a forest fire) may lie within nature, the consequences of the event are never strictly within nature, which is true of all natural disasters. This is because the response to the disaster involves people, organizations, and systems that are subject to finances, policies, politics, and culture.[28] People evaluate these factors as they assess the consequences they experienced from the disaster. They think about the timeliness of disaster response, the fair distribution of relief, when subsequent services are expected, and more. All these issues impact a survivor's experience of a disaster and the type and degree of consequences they experience.

Lidskog goes on to cite evidence for the fact that the way people evaluate disasters falls into two broad patterns: therapeutic or corrosive. A therapeutic pattern emerges when people in the community respond in altruistic ways, pulling together and helping one another through the event. Alternatively, disasters can cause a corrosive pattern of social rupture, where people devolve into blame, attacks, and conflict. One of the clearest descriptions of this negative response to disaster is by Miller,[29] who returned home after Hurricane Katrina to find that his community had devolved into loss of community trust, loss of social capital, and loss of interaction between neighbors. One of the most striking indicators of this loss of trust was the posting of signs throughout the area warning against criminal activity.

These two patterns described by Lidskog predict future resilience. A therapeutic response leads to positive appraisals of the community and assumptions that the community members care for and will help one another. These positive assumptions predict future positive behavior. Conversely, negative assumptions predict future negative behavior. People with no expectations of being helped in their time of need will tend to mistrust others as well as look out only for themselves. The marks of a non-resilient community are a failure to respond to those in need and division of the community into groups that maintain their separate subcommunities.

Consider this alternative scenario. In the fall of 2018, a major fire destroyed 90 percent of the town of Paradise, California. After this catastrophe, many stories emerged about people helping one another. One story, that became

---

28. Lidskog, 16.
29. Miller, "Visualizing the Corrosive Community," 71–73.

national news, was about a garbage-truck driver who heard that an older woman on his route had not evacuated and had no way to get out. At great personal risk, he got in his truck and drove through the fire to rescue her. Stories like this quickly circulate and send the message that this is a community where people can be trusted to help one another. The local citizens repeated this story many times when they spoke with news reporters. This is a town where trust has grown and where people are more likely to work together when the next disaster strikes.

These stories also illustrate other aspects of responses that build trust. In addition to responding to fellow citizens in need, the responders acted in a timely way, served people based only on the urgency of their needs, and made resources available in an equitable way. People assess the response to a disaster according to what they see as a just response – that is, services to people are consistent with what community members see as reflecting justice. Thus, trust builds when people see that they receive justice; it declines when services violate standards for justice. We look more closely at this in the next section.

Loss of trust as the root of the breakdown of social capital and subsequent breakdown of resilience is consistent with reports from other disasters. For example, Mayer et al. describe how, following the Deepwater Horizon oil spill, a poorly managed and inequitable compensation system led to competition and distrust among community members that frayed the social fabric and was ultimately destructive to the communities.[30] Likewise, Messer et al.[31] describe how a toxic spill led to community conflict and distrust. People closest to the toxic spill perceived a greater threat to their health compared with those further away from the spill. The citizens' different levels of trust in the organization responsible for the spill grew into distrust and then antagonism between groups of people. These conflicts had significant and potentially long-lasting negative impacts on the quality of community relations.

As mentioned, these trust issues appear linked to justice. In the examples of community conflict, there is not just distrust but, more specifically, distrust about whether an organization, group, or government will act in a just manner. In the case of the toxic spill, people closest to the spill had a greater sense of threat and loss, as well as heightened concern over whether they would receive just treatment. Messer and colleagues say that the people further from the spill perceived those who were protesting against the organization as troublemakers who were harming the community with their protests. Both

30. Mayer et al., "Compensation and Community Corrosion."
31. Messer, Shriver, and Kennedy, "Environmental Hazards."

groups saw the issue as one of harm and injustice. Because they lacked a trusted broker for the conflict, the two camps ended up "hunkering down for a long and protracted battle."[32] In such a divided community, it is easy to see how community cooperation and support is lost and the community is less prepared for a subsequent disaster.

Resilience and the Just Community

It is common to think of justice as the administration of consequences for breaking the law. Justice, however, takes many forms. Social justice is the view that everyone deserves equal economic, political, and social rights and opportunities. Procedural justice is about the fair process of administering justice and settling disputes. Distributive justice is the just allocation of goods and the reduction of inequality. Retributive justice is concerned with making the punishment proportionate to the crime. Restorative justice addresses repairing the harm caused by others. Contributive justice speaks of the responsibility to benefit society. What each of these forms of justice has in common is a sense of "ought" – that this is the way things ought to be. The range of justice types shows how broadly we apply this sense of "ought" and the wide variety of ways in which we may encounter issues of justice when it comes to complicated events like a disaster and restoration following damage and loss.

Historically, issues of compensation, fair distribution of goods, and social rights were seen as expressions of a basic self-interest motive. Psychology traditionally maintained that people are fundamentally motivated by self-interest and getting what is due to them. Lerner and Clayton challenged this self-interest approach by suggesting that justice is a basic human drive in its own right, *along* with self-interest, rather than only an expression of self-interest.[33] An inherent view of justice suggests that people have a strong desire to see the world as a just place. When people experience injustice toward themselves or others, it creates dissonance. Dissonance is a tension that exists when two incompatible experiences exist together. In this case, it is the tension between believing the world is just and seeing injustice. This tension has a variety of social and behavioral consequences, including retaliation against those who cause injustice. For example, in a study of the LFC and justice in a refugee camp, Boan et al. found that perceived distributive injustice was

---

32. Messer, Shriver, and Kennedy, 180.
33. Lerner and Clayton, *Justice and Self-Interest*.

perpetuating conflict between groups in a refugee camp.[34] The camp fits our earlier description of a corrosive pattern in a community. There existed widespread distrust and the expectation of injustice in relationships between members of the community. When an LFC network that dedicated itself to establishing justice was formed, the conflict declined significantly and the camp became more successful at resolving subsequent conflicts. This story illustrates the connection between justice and conflict, as well as between justice and community resilience, when faced with adversity. Communities are primed for conflict when there is an expectation of injustice. In such situations, small events become explosive because they confirm the belief in injustice. Where trust exists, then justice is assumed, and small events can be contained and resolved before they become explosive.

When our sense of justice creates tension because we are faced with an injustice, we have a choice between two courses of action: We may either act on behalf of the victim and see that they receive justice, or we may reinterpret the event in a way that says there was no injustice. Reinterpreting the event generally means finding a way to say that the victim is not a victim after all because, for some reason, they deserve what happened. Reinterpreting results in the all-too-familiar attitude of blaming the victim, which takes many forms: the poor deserve their fate because they are lazy; victims of a crime failed to take care to avoid exposure to criminal areas; we should not provide aid to poorer countries because people will just become dependent. These and other excuses are the greatest barriers to compassion toward individuals and communities because they justify inaction. LFCs planning to increase community engagement will need to recognize these barriers and be prepared to counter them. We will take this up when we discuss recommended actions.

Trust and justice are related. Justice builds trust, reduces the risk of conflict, and creates confidence that community procedures will be fair. As shown in the example from Kakuma (in chapter 3), a church network can model many forms of justice and demonstrate to the community how justice benefits everyone.

Resilience and the Conservation of Resources

The conservation of resources (COR) theory proposes that the impact of a disaster event on an individual is related to the degree of resource loss. COR is a model that is related to concepts of social capital (discussed later) and social vulnerability (discussed below). It states that resources come in many

---

34. Boan et al., "Qualitative Study."

forms and include such things as material and social resources, personal skills, physical attributes, and more. Particularly for those with fewer material resources, the community itself becomes an important resource.[35] There is a considerable body of evidence of the direct relationship between loss and the severity of the resulting trauma.[36] The COR theory has held up in studies of a variety of disasters and conflicts – including natural disasters, violence, war, and technical disasters – and across a variety of national and cultural settings. One conclusion from the COR theory is that whatever facilitates the access to resources, mitigates the loss of resources, and aids in their recovery will aid individual and community resilience. Here is an area of influence for the LFC and local NGOs – restoring lost resources.

One example of the importance of resource loss comes from a study carried out by Snyder, Boan, Davis, and Aten in the North Kivu region of the Democratic Republic of the Congo.[37] North Kivu is an area that has seen ongoing violence since the mid-1990s. The conflict displaced hundreds of thousands of people, many of them multiple times. The study asked: What do people lose in a situation like this and what is the impact on their physical and mental health? The study also looked at over a hundred LFC leaders, their role in the community, and their physical and mental health. Over four hundred people completed interviews about their health and mental health symptoms, trauma, extent and types of losses, and the nature and frequency of displacement. The findings revealed that both mental and physical health symptoms, including trauma symptoms, were directly related to the type and extent of losses. Of particular concern was the impact on LFC leaders. As people suffered losses and repeated violence, they turned to LFC leaders for help. These pastors, most of whom had little or no formal training, felt unprepared to minister to the needs of a community of suffering people. As a result, the study revealed, the pastors displayed more severe symptoms than the average non-pastor. Not only did the pastors suffer the same exposure to violence and loss, they also endured the experience of feeling ill-equipped to care for the members of their community, which led some to question their faith and trust in God's provision. This illustrates how losses cascade. The pastors suffered the initial loss of family and property, then experienced the loss of their sense of adequacy when faced with people in need, and finally, the loss of faith. In one meeting, in response to someone who suggested that

---

35. Cox and Perry, "Like a Fish."
36. Hobfoll and Lilly, "Resource Conservation."
37. Snyder et al., "Resource Loss."

the LFC leaders needed to pray, a pastor said, "Maybe you know another God we can pray to as ours does not seem to be listening." Their sense of despair was symptomatic of what the majority in the community were experiencing.

These studies led to the development of a unique set of community intervention methods that emphasize protecting people from loss and aiding them in recovering from loss as soon as possible. For community members, this can mean quickly reestablishing community connections, replacing lost equipment, or reconnecting family members. For example, in DR Congo the loss of farming utensils was one of the most significant. This loss threatened a family's ability to feed itself. Simply replacing the lost items can lower the daily distress experienced by a family and thereby also reduce other health symptoms. In the case of pastors, the recommendation was to create a network of faith leaders who will support one another and then train the network in practical support methods they can use when community members are traumatized.

Since restoring lost resources appears to be an important strategy for the care of those suffering a major loss, imagine the consequences when restoring resources is seen as failing the justice test. Injustice happens in some communities where LFCs volunteer to serve as distributors of community aid but, perhaps without thinking of the greater consequences, focus on their members first. Prioritizing its interests has led to charges that the LFCs involved do not care about those in need but only want to invest in their supporters. Being perceived as unjust is very destructive for an LFC and harmful to the entire community, and this perception, once established, is very difficult to change.

Several international studies examine the role of the LFC as a community resource. For example, Rich, Sirikantraporn, and Jean-Charles surveyed survivors of the Haiti earthquake, asking about the role of the LFC and faith.[38] They found that, during a disaster, respondents relied on their faith in two important ways: First, as a source of coping and aid to recovery; second, for the sense of not being alone. People reported that the LFC helped them cope with life problems "because they got to know about other people's struggles, which they know they were not alone in the struggles and life's hardships."[39]

Since they are important resources, faith and connection to a faith community are both vulnerable to loss and also capable of being restored. Seeing faith as a resource begins to shed light on the special role a faith community can play, a role that is unique to that community when it bolsters

---

38. Rich, Sirikantraporn, and Jean-Charles, "Post-Traumatic Growth."
39. Rich, Sirikantraporn, and Jean-Charles, 33.

existing faith resources and comes alongside people who feel that their faith is threatened or lost as a result of a crisis. It is a concept that we will continue to develop as we go forward.

Resilience, the Ecological Model and the LFC

The social-ecological model emphasizes the social context in creating resilience. It asserts that we must understand the context a person lives in if we are to understand resilience. In this view, personal factors are still important, but these can only be properly understood when considered as part of an interaction between the individual and the larger community. The concept of social vulnerability to harm illustrates this interaction.

Susan Cutter and her colleagues' influential work on social vulnerability used national-level data to develop an empirical model of vulnerability to community harm in a disaster.[40] Their model predicted the potential to suffer loss in a disaster and to experience longer and more complicated recovery. The social vulnerability model is, effectively, the antithesis of resilience. It shows how limited resources and limited access to available resources increases the harm a community will experience when exposed to a disaster event. Later work also showed that similar disaster events produce different levels of harm relative to the levels of social vulnerability. Not only is harm related to vulnerability, but vulnerability is largely the product of social factors that determine distribution and access to resources. In effect, vulnerability and the related potential to suffer harm in a disaster are partly a function of social inequality.[41] As such, social vulnerability is related to social justice. As Cutter notes:

> Social vulnerability is partially the product of social inequalities – those social factors that influence or shape the susceptibility of various groups to harm and that also govern their ability to respond. However, it also includes place inequalities – those characteristics of communities and the built environment, such as the level of urbanization, growth rates, and economic vitality, that contribute to the social vulnerability of places.[42]

Ecological models – such as the social vulnerability model – describe protective factors as well as vulnerability factors and losses that mediate the

---

40. Cutter, Boruff and Shirley, "Social Vulnerability."
41. Cutter and Emrich, "Moral Hazard," 102.
42. Cutter, Boruff, and Shirley, "Social Vulnerability," 243.

impact of disasters. These models led to work on the concept of community protective factors that are especially important in poorly-resourced communities with vulnerable populations, some of which do not exist in the West.[43] An ecological view accounts for these multiple factors and how they interact over time. Building on the work of Urie Bronfenbrenner, Ungar emphasizes that resilience is not only about personal factors but also the availability of resources and the ability of individuals to access and make use of the resources.[44] He describes seven factors that result in an environment that enhances protective factors for development.[45] These are:

- Access to material resources (e.g. economic opportunity, education, information,[46] access to food, clothing, and shelter). Here, we add access to information – LFCs often serve as the central information gathering and dissemination point for communities. Access is critically important in slow-onset shocks and stresses like drought, where early warning information helps determine when to plant and harvest or when to vaccinate, destock herds, and more. Likewise, LFCs often have the resources necessary to purchase radio and other communication equipment and will thus receive early warning messages even for quick-onset disasters like storms/typhoons.
- Relationships (connections with meaningful others, family, the community at large).
- Identity (a sense of purpose, beliefs, and values, including spiritual and religious identification).
- Power (the ability to effect change, access resources).
- Cultural adherence (adherence to values and beliefs).
- Social justice (meaningful role in the community and social equality).
- Cohesion (balancing personal interest with a sense of responsibility to the greater good; feeling a part of something larger than oneself, socially and spiritually).[47]

---

43. Ungar, Ghazinour, and Richter, "Annual Research Review."

44. Ungar, *Social Ecology of Resilience*.

45. Ungar, Ghazinour, and Richter, "Annual Research Review."

46. Information was not part of the Ungar model, but the authors consider it an important addition. Engaging people with information, facilitating processing of that information and, in some cases, acquiring tools needed for information access (e.g. radios) is a critical LFC function.

47. Ungar, Ghazinour, and Richter, "Annual Research Review," 351.

In these and other elements of the ecological approach to resilience, we see a link to the LFC and its ministries (next section) and can begin to construct a broader role for the LFC in developing a strong community. As we will discuss later, most of the elements of the ecological model are associated with social capital. Having access to resources requires a social infrastructure that facilitates that access. Relationships are social capital, and fostering identity and promoting community power (that is, people's interactions with their community which help them to be effective and meet their needs) are important elements of social capital, as are social justice and cohesion.

Other authors have proposed models that challenge conventional conceptions of resilience by emphasizing a broader, more integrative view of resilience, which is embedded primarily in the community rather than within individuals. Djalante and colleagues propose what they call "adaptive and integrative disaster resilience (AIDR)" where

> AIDR provides the ability to face complexities and uncertainties by designing institutional processes that function across sectors and scales, to engage multiple stakeholders and to promote social learning.[48]

The proposed model from Djalante et al. has an institutional and organizational emphasis that differs from the developmental focus of the ecological model. They describe institutional pathways to AIDR that have implications for the LFC as well as for other community institutions:

- strengthening governance
- fostering collaborations
- improving knowledge and information
- enabling institutional learning
- self-organization and networking
- provision of disaster finance[49]

These elements are the structural side of the social and structural components of social capital. Strengthening governance has both an internal (for example, responsible LFC leaders) and an external (for example, holding government accountable) side. Fostering collaboration, like improving knowledge and information, is a process that builds social capital. The other

---

48. Djalante et al., "Pathways," 2105.
49. Djalante et al., 2105–2135.

elements speak to building the structures needed to support social capital – which could be described as providing the scaffolding for social networks.

A third prominent model is that by Norris and her colleagues, who describe community resilience as the result of a set of networked adaptive capacities. Her model stresses the adaptive aspect:

> This is an important point: resilience rests on both the resources themselves and the dynamic attributes of those resources (robustness, redundancy, rapidity); we use the term "adaptive capacities" to capture this combination.[50]

There are four adaptive capacities – with "adaptive" meaning that they are dynamic – that underpin resilience: (1) information and communication, (2) economic development, (3) social capital, and (4) community competence. Looking more closely at these four capacities, we begin to see where the LFC would play an important role. Information and communication include having a trusted media, developing skills for communicating and using information, and having trusted sources of information. "Community competence" refers to collective action, problem-solving, empowerment, and political partnerships. Social capital, as Norris uses it, includes support, attachment, cooperation, link to place, and a sense of community. Finally, economic development emphasizes fairness, equitable distribution, and diversity in resources.

These models (institutional, developmental, and dynamic) find support in the current literature. Sherrieb et al. tested the Norris framework in New Orleans after Hurricane Katrina and found that the four capacities were associated with greater recovery from the disaster, along with higher levels of health and mental health.[51] The necessity for inclusive collaboration, both across the community and between local and national or international agencies, is a clear theme in the literature.[52]

Resilience, Social Capital, and the LFC

Social justice is another repeated theme, with community groups dedicated to ensuring representation of marginalized groups.

> A social justice perspective that attends to the needs and voices of marginalized groups is essential [for a healthy community],

---

50. Norris et al., "Community Resilience," 135.
51. Sherrieb, Norris, and Galea, "Measuring Capacities."
52. Bava et al., "Lessons in Collaboration."

even if this perspective puts collaboration in conflict with local authorities who do not have this as a priority.[53]

Others have taken the social justice issue further by asserting that social equity is essential for development and resilience. Benner and Pastor write that tight integration between equity, development, and resilience occurs to the extent that communities emphasize collaboration, inclusiveness, and equity.[54] These communities demonstrate superior rates of growth and sustainable resilience. In such communities, people have a shared sense of destiny that unites them and promotes a more inclusive and constructive approach to conflict.

> Such knowledge communities, in short, provide exactly the norms, standards and (place) identity that are the micro-foundations for linking equity and growth: because there is genuine care for the other, partly because of the communicative processes inherent in such communities, economic and social actors look for "win-win" opportunities rather than Darwinian competitive destruction.[55]

"Social capital" refers to the social relationships, and the resources and information exchanged through that network of relationships – including social norms and trust – that facilitate individual or community action.[56] Newton adds that social capital focuses on the cultural values and attitudes that encourage citizens within a community to cooperate, trust, understand, and empathize with one another.[57] It is helpful, in any discussion of social capital, to draw out a few nuances – namely, the nature of "strong and weak ties"[58] and the triad of bonding, bridging, and linking social capital[59] – in order to understand the positive and negative features of social capital.[60] The case study from Lebanon (in chapter 5) illustrates the effectiveness of LFCs in helping to build social cohesion in a rapidly changing environment as Lebanese societies continue to receive and host Syrian refugees.

---

53. Bava et al., 547.

54. Benner and Pastor, "Whither Resilience Regions?"

55. Benner and Pastor, 20.

56. Bourdieu, "Forms of Capital"; Coleman, "Social Capital"; Putnam, *Bowling Alone*.

57. Newton, "Social Capital and Democracy."

58. Granovetter, "Strength of Weak Ties."

59. Gittell and Vidal, *Community Organizing*; Aldrich, *Building Resilience*.

60. Chambers and Kopstein, "Bad Civil Society."

Strong and Weak Ties

The sociologist Mark Granovetter is well known for developing a nomenclature of "strong and weak ties" to describe the qualities of social connections based on the frequency and nature of interactions and on the expectations from those ties. He argues, "the strength of a tie is a (probably linear) combination of the amount of time, the emotional intensity, the intimacy (mutual confiding), and the reciprocal services which characterize the tie."[61] Strong ties are often found in close-knit, typically smaller, denser networks that are characterized by more frequent interactions. As such, these stronger ties often consume and require more time, which usually results in fewer ties of this sort.

Weak ties, then, are typically connections between people who belong to much more distant points in a network, with fewer interactions with one another, yet often containing qualitatively and quantitatively different resources that are useful for recovery from shocks and stresses. Beggs et al. agree: "Weak ties are likely to be found in networks or portions of networks of high range" and "are more likely to link dissimilar individuals, to connect individuals to more diverse parts of the social structure and, therefore, to provide access to the non-redundant information that leads to successful instrumental action."[62] "Intuitively speaking, this means that whatever is to be diffused can reach a larger number of people, and traverse a greater social distance (i.e., path length), when passed through weak ties rather than strong."[63] Naturally, weaker ties tend to introduce an individual to others less like himself and with access to different assets and information.

Bonding, Bridging, and Linking Social Capital

Those with whom we share strong ties "tend to be concentrated within particular groups."[64] Bonding social capital happens within groups of "immediate family members, neighbors, close friends, and business associates sharing similar demographic characteristics,"[65] a common purpose,[66] norms of trust, and a "shared membership and identity," which "provide members a sense of belongingness."[67] "Bonding social capital constitutes a kind of sociological

---

61. Granovetter, "Strength of Weak Ties," 1361.
62. Beggs, Haines, and Hurlbert, "Situational Contingencies," 205.
63. Granovetter, "Strength of Weak Ties," 1366.
64. Granovetter, 1376.
65. Nakagawa and Shaw, "Social Capital," 8.
66. Carron and Brawley, "Cohesion."
67. Lin, "Network Theory."

superglue."[68] Here, it is helpful to discuss Carron and Brawley's influential work on cohesion. While not directly analogous to bonding social capital, cohesion may be defined as "the tendency for a group to stick together and remain united in the pursuit of its instrumental objectives and for the satisfaction of member affective needs."[69] Cohesion depends on the beliefs of group members about "its closeness, similarity, and bonding as a whole and the degree of unification of the group" and "the individual's personal motivations to remain in the group."[70] In short, groups that display high levels of cohesion and unity are likely to be more tightly "bonded" and, therefore, will find bonding social capital more abundant and easier to access and utilize than groups with lower cohesion and unity levels.

Naturally, for the LFC, bonding social capital comes relatively easily and is abundant. For example, individual Christian churches exhibit a shared purpose, membership, identity, and unity that center on faith in Jesus Christ. LFCs exhibit and create social capital by bringing together people who share a common faith and values, and building relationships among them. In the process, people learn about the content of their faith identity and how that identity relates to the larger world – hence the need for a theological framework for engagement.

Bridging social capital is found in relationships between networks or groups who do not share a common identity or membership. The term "bridging" is metaphorically appropriate as it explains the act of spanning a river, partition, or divide. As opposed to bonded groups, bridged relationships span group boundaries horizontally, putting people into contact with "others" unlike themselves. It "comprises relations of respect and mutuality between people who know that they are not alike in some sociodemographic (or social identity) sense (differing by age, ethnic group, class, etc)."[71] The reasons for social engagement remain the same: to secure additional resources and perform collective actions otherwise impossible individually. However, bridging social capital provides access to new, diverse resources and collective action[72] and allows individuals to "draw on these links when local resources are insufficient or unavailable."[73]

---

68. Putnam, *Bowling Alone*, 23.

69. Carron and Brawley, "Cohesion."

70. Carron and Brawley, 727.

71. Szreter and Woolcock, "Health by Association?," 656.

72. Szreter, "State of Social Capital."

73. Wetterberg, "Crisis, Social Ties," 7.

In many cases, members of tightly bonded LFCs also engage in other aspects of the community – such as civic groups, public office, or other economic or community organizations. In the process, they bring their beliefs and values into the public sphere. When these values include care and advocacy for the vulnerable, service for those in need, justice, advocacy, or other services to the community, then community resilience grows. Not only does resilience in terms of disaster resilience grow, but more fundamentally, the community becomes a healthier and more prosperous place. Community resilience is especially present when community engagement empowers others and brings down barriers between different populations within the community.

Linking social capital is "vertical" in the sense that it does not describe peer-to-peer horizontal relationships or networks but refers to networks which span "vertically," connecting actors "across explicit, formal or institutionalized power or authority gradients in society."[74] The engagement of LFCs with linking social capital takes place in two forms: (1) as a civil society organism interacting with government entities and other public and private entities with power, authority, and resources greater than itself, and (2) as a member of a larger denominational network with hierarchical structures reaching to the national, regional, and, in many cases, international level. The contribution of the LFC, in terms of linking social capital, then takes the form of a coalition for a shared, greater, and more powerful voice in public affairs. Advocacy can include the defense of the voiceless or powerless, and the channeling of resources (financial, human, and otherwise) from higher levels to the community level, as well as a rich contribution to higher denominational levels of testimony and witness to God's work in the community.

Some of the strongest examples of this come from the Christian church's response to violence in Syria and Iraq. In Syria, several Greek Orthodox churches and Syriac Orthodox churches, along with several other churches, formed the International Orthodox Christian Charities (IOCC) to provide life-saving humanitarian aid to displaced Syrians inside the country as well as to Syrian refugees outside of Syria. These networks then banded together with Catholic networks for increased scope and scale. In Iraq, "following the massive wave of internal displacement in 2014, a new Council of Churches was established which coordinates aid to displaced families of all religious backgrounds in Christian villages. When interfaith conflicts arise, Iraqi Christian community leaders have engaged members of the local Muslim

---

74. Szreter and Woolcock, "Health by Association?," 656.

communities to discuss prevention and cooperation."[75] These forms of the LFC's contribution to resilience are explored in more detail elsewhere in this book.

Social capital is not, however, without its dangers. Chambers and Kopstein, in their seminal work *Bad Civil Society*, discuss the discriminatory selection of whom these self-serving "bad" groups choose to help. Tightly-bonded groups become exclusive, "defensive, sect-line," and "profoundly divisive and separatist,"[76] which "may impede the articulation of collective interests and the development of extensive bridging and linking social capital."[77] Naturally, individuals find it easier and more comfortable to connect with and bond with people who are most like themselves. Conversely, bridging social capital requires a lot of effort and focused energy to overcome language, social distance, and cultural barriers to develop beneficial networks. Therefore, bridging social capital is not easily developed. Discrimination is perhaps the most accurate antithesis to bridging social capital. Timothy Gill, in his research on caste-based exclusivity following the December 2004 tsunami, cites multiple consequences of a lack of bridging social capital. Difficulties in bridging social boundaries resulted in "rice thrown in the sea rather than given to Dalit victims," refusal to provide Dalits with proper protective equipment while clearing dead bodies and human waste, "using the tsunami to evict an entire Dalit community," and exclusion of the Dalit community by the local churches.[78] In the end, power and strongly bonded social ties allowed dominant castes to exclude, oppress, and take advantage of the Dalit community.

The marginalized Dalits found it difficult or nearly impossible to bridge or link with higher level, more powerful networks. "Linking social capital, it should be added, like bonding and bridging, can also be put to unhappy purposes – e.g., nepotism, corruption, and suppression."[79] A lack of accountability of the socially well-connected allows them to abdicate any political responsibility to their marginalized constituencies. Szreter and Woolcock warn that "without attention to the quality of the relationships between those with differential access to power . . . efforts at poverty alleviation, economic development, and service provision to the poor are unlikely to succeed."[80] Additionally, "If the

---

75. Kraft and Manar, "Hope for the Middle East," 14.
76. Szreter, "State of Social Capital," 585.
77. Szreter and Woolcock, "Health by Association?," 660.
78. Gill, *Making Things Worse*, 29, 31, 36, 41.
79. Szreter and Woolcock, "Health by Association?," 656.
80. Szreter and Woolcock, 657.

first individual can satisfy his need through self-sufficiency, or aid from some official source without incurring an obligation, he will do so – and thus fail to add to the social capital outstanding in the community."[81]

When participation in the LFC is accompanied by promoting separation from community, isolation, or dividing the community into more and less acceptable members, then community resilience does not improve. Resilience may decline as a result of reinforcing barriers between people, and those in need go without advocates. In one sense, this is the battle against homophily – the tendency of people to relate mainly to those like themselves. Community resilience requires lower boundaries between groups and a related sense of a common identity based in the community or a common bond as members of God's creation.

Some writers speak to this issue of the impact inherent in how the LFC relates to the broader community. Kame and Tshaka describe the LFC as a unique civil institution with a necessary role in community justice.[82] They describe the rise of economic corruption (inequality being one form of corruption) as being due not to a failure of systems or leadership but to a more fundamental decline in moral and spiritual values. What was formerly known as the "Protestant work ethic" provided this framework, but in the modern world that ethic is no longer considered relevant. Thus, they argue that LFCs need to be at the center of a reassertion of moral social values, including economic values, that put forward a new moral economic framework for modern society. They further assert that such a refocusing will reinvigorate the LFC with a greater sense of relevance at a time when the LFC in the West is in decline.[83] This theme is also described by Brown and Brown, who stress that what is needed from the LFC is not just taking a stand on issues but establishing the role of the LFC in seeking a better society by strengthening society's moral foundation.[84] The implication is that when the LFC engages in a meaningful way with injustice in the community, both the LFC and the community benefit.

So how does an LFC strengthen the community's moral foundation? Focusing on economic issues and injustice, Powelson describes a just and moral economy as one where there is a culture of moral economic behavior[85] –

---

81. Coleman, "Social Capital."
82. Kame and Tshaka, "Morality and Spirituality."
83. Kame and Tshaka.
84. Brown and Brown, "Faith and Works."
85. Powelson, *Moral Economy*.

that is, one where institutions (e.g. LFCs) make moral assertions (engage in public discourse) that offset the concentration of power with elites. In such an economy, "religion provides the means for internalizing the rules of proper market behavior."[86] Thus, a moral economy depends on strong institutions that assert moral values and influence culture away from the excesses of a purely market-driven economy. This view of institutions and their importance for both the economy and for democracy is echoed by Calhoun, who states that "a vibrant public sphere is the dimension of civil society most essential to democracy."[87] Bruyn makes a similar assertion, namely that civil society, as envisioned by Adam Smith, is one where institutions cooperate to create systems of social accountability.[88] Bruyn contrasts this with the current state (as of 1999), where people too often view others as threats to their self-interest. What is needed to counter this loss of civil society is a "third sector" that serves the interests of those people not served by either the government or the private sector. Bruyn describes this third sector as the not-for-profit realm. We assert that it is also the role of the LFC. Only the LFC brings a moral framework for engagement in the community, which is precisely the argument (above) of Kame and Tshaka.[89] Civic engagement, however, will mean a shift for many LFCs – from a personal service focus to a community and civic institutions focus such as influencing policy, advocating for the vulnerable, and political activism.

Resilience, Spiritual Integration, and the LFC

The work on personal resilience is taken further by the concept of resilience as a spiritual adaptation. Doehring writes that resilience is neither strictly personal nor a fixed trait, but rooted in dynamic and relational processes that either support or interfere with the ability to cope with adversity.[90] This view starts with the observation that conflict and distress have a moral component. When an experience conflicts with a person's commitments and beliefs, either from their own behavior or from being exposed to a conflicting event, it produces spiritual distress that reduces their ability to cope. We see examples of this in people of faith who experience severe violence that undermines their sense of a compassionate God, or military people who experience "moral injury"

86. Powelson, 175.

87. Calhoun, "Civil Society," 18.

88. Bruyn, "Moral Economy," 25.

89. Kame and Tshaka, "Morality and Spirituality."

90. Doehring, "Resilience as the Relational Ability."

as a result of their actions while in deployment. When people have access to compassionate and spiritual care, they have a far greater ability to cope with adversity.

While this model focuses more on personal coping, it adopts more of a contextual view than other psychological models. It fits into a social capital model where access to resources, including spiritual resources, is critical to the ability to resist and recover from harm. It fits with the view that while some faith perspectives support adaptation and coping, other faith perspectives reduce resilience. For example, we know that people who view God as compassionate have more resilience, as shown by their ability to recover sooner compared with people with a view of God as judge. In this view, the LFC has multiple roles. It creates a capacity for resilience through the development of spiritual strengths and assists in coping and recovery through compassionate caring.

We see the aforementioned perspectives on resilience coming together in what is called a multidimensional view of resilience.

A Multidimensional Model of Resilience and the LFC

As the name suggests, the multidimensional view seeks to integrate various resilience factors into a comprehensive model. The advantage of broad models of this type is that they tend to be a better reflection of how the real world functions. Smith et al. note that their work on the floods in Bangladesh highlights the need for a comprehensive and multidimensional approach to resilience in order to account for the variety of capacities that are related to overall resilience.[91] Further, they call for additional research that reflects this comprehensive approach. Given that in the academic and research worlds there is a tendency to fragment the natural and social worlds into units that are easier to study, their recommendation is important. Fragmentation helps make a study more manageable but at the cost of losing our sense of the extent to which different parts of our world interact.

Several researchers support a multidimensional view of resilience[92] due to the connections they see between multiple resilience factors and thriving,[93]

---

91. Smith and Frankenberger, "Does Resilience Capacity?"

92. IFRC, "Characteristics"; Mayunga, "Understanding and Applying"; Narayan et al., *Voices of the Poor.*

93. Wulff et al., "What Is Health Resilience?"

mental health in youth,[94] managing financial stress,[95] social connections facilitating diversification of resources, livelihoods, and assets,[96] the importance of resilience for adaptation to climate change,[97] political and social acceptance of displaced people and that community's resilience,[98] religion and the idea of the sacred in violence prevention and peacebuilding,[99] racism,[100] the intersection of social learning, social memory and leadership for self-organization,[101] personal relationships, homelessness,[102] the importance of gender as a cross-cutting issue,[103] the intersection of relief and development activities[104] and many, many others. For a comprehensive and thorough treatment of the multidimensional nature of resilience, refer to Twigg's *Characteristics of a Disaster Resilience Community* (2009) and International Federation of the Red Cross's (IFRC) subsequent *Characteristics of a Safe and Resilience Community* (2011).

A multidimensional model also highlights the breadth of resilience and its importance in many aspects of life. As Wulf et al. note, " a community resilience paradigm can help communities and individuals not just to mitigate damage and heal, but to thrive."[105] We extend this importance to faith communities whose role in the community extends far beyond disaster response.[106] This model of resilience begins to treat resources in less reductive ways (i.e. avoiding the simple, direct formula that more resources equals more resilience) and begins to explore the multifaceted and complex ways in which these resources are utilized and combined and the various obstacles or "unfreedoms"[107] that prevent effective resource utilization. The real "art" of resilience consists of the

---

94. Fritz et al., "Systemic Review," 230.

95. Doehring and Arora, "Spiritually-Integrated Financial Resilience."

96. Adger, "Social and Ecological Resilience"; Adger et al., "Migration, Remittances"; Aldrich, *Building Resilience*.

97. Adger, "Social Capital."

98. Aldrich and Crook, "Strong Civil Society;" Dynes and Quarantelli, "Brief Note," 1–5; Portes and Sensenbrenner, "Embeddedness and Immigration."

99. Appleby, "Ambivalence of the Sacred."

100. Brown and Brown, "Faith and Works."

101. Berkes, "Understanding Uncertainty"; Cutter et al., "Place-Based Model"; Folke, "Resilience: The Emergence."

102. Dordick, *Something Left to Lose*.

103. Djupe et al., "Present but Not Accounted For?"

104. IFRC, "The Road to Resilience."

105. Wulff et al., "What Is Health Resilience?," 361.

106. Deneulin and Bano, *Religion in Development*; Haynes, *Religion and Development*; Todd, *Fast Living*.

107. Sen, *Development as Freedom*.

skills and creativity that inform the employment of resources for recovery – in what combinations, quantities, and methods, and for precisely what purposes.

The LFC has an indirect (and sometimes direct) influence on the employment of resources and capital by individuals and on the collective response to, and recovery from, disasters, shocks, and stresses. The ways in which we use and interact with the natural environment, individually and communally, in the pursuit of our individual and common good directly impact our vulnerabilities to future natural hazards and capacities to respond to and recover from them. Indeed, our use and misuse of natural resources can create or prolong natural hazards and instigate conflict between those vying for scarce resources.

The LFC speaks directly to the moral, ethical, and spiritual uses of resources for the common good. In response to an event, there are numerous different ways to utilize resources. This brings into the equation issues of collective action and the common good – how people choose to employ resources (personal, communal, or those of others) for their own recovery or that of the community has a direct bearing on others' resilience, and vice versa, particularly in an ever-changing environment. The nature, quantity, and quality of resources at a person's disposal change frequently – sometimes daily – for the poorest, most vulnerable groups in a community. Nature and severity of life events can vary greatly from event to event. Likewise, the frequency at which cyclical events strike can have serious implications on what an individual or community has on hand for response and recovery. If most of our resources are consumed to recover from this year's drought event, what happens next year or the year after that? All of this assumes that the goal is to return to the *ex-ante* state, before the shock or stress. This is *absorptive capacity* – how much of the shock or stress can be "absorbed" without a fundamental change or failure to return to the *ex-ante* condition without making significant changes to one's life or community. For example, rice farmers vulnerable to drought may save a portion of their proceeds and invest a portion in crop insurance but continue the essentials of rice farming.

The next level, called *adaptive capacity,* is just what the name implies – if the shock or stress exceeds the ability to absorb the impacts in their various forms, then adaptation of activities, methods, approaches, and systems is required to operate in the *new reality* and to continue functioning despite uncertainty – for example, begin planting more drought-tolerant rice, install an irrigation system, and shift planting and harvesting periods by a few weeks.

Transformative capacity is the ultimate resilience capacity – the capacity to fundamentally change the very form and nature of life, the deep structures and systems that cause or increase vulnerability and risk, and the way societies share risk by addressing underlying failures of development and power imbalances that cause, increase, or maintain risk and poverty. Transforming society has, perhaps, been the most significant and lasting contribution of the LFC to the world over the past two millennia. Transformation of individuals and peoples at large requires the change of the very beliefs, attitudes, worldviews, and resultant systems and interpersonal dynamics that created the vulnerabilities and poverty we seek to address. While the Christian church can certainly contribute to its community's ability to absorb or even adapt to various shocks or stresses, its ability to support and facilitate true human, social, and political transformation through the redeeming and reconciling work of Jesus Christ and the Holy Spirit is critical, and should be supported and encouraged.

2

Theological Models

Resilience and Integral Mission

In this section, we consider models for a theology of LFC engagement in the community that builds community health and resilience. Engaging with the community in a way that builds peace and health aligns closely with integral mission. Therefore, we start with a summary of integral mission and present excerpts from Rene Padilla's writing on the ecclesiology of integral mission.[1]

Padilla starts by listing the basic requirements for a Christian church to practice integral mission. These are:

- A commitment to Christ as Lord of everything. This is to recognize Christ as sovereign over all of creation. This means that the kingdom of God is a present reality in the person of Christ. Padilla notes that Christianity has emphasized Christology over ecclesiology. A proper balance comes from an LFC as a community that professes and proclaims Jesus as Lord of creation. The integral LFC lives this by seeing all spheres of life as mission fields and by looking for ways to assert the sovereignty of Christ in all of them.[2]

- Discipleship is a missionary lifestyle of active participation in God's plan for creation. This is the essence of the mission of the LFC.[3] This is balancing orthodoxy (right belief) with orthopraxis (living out the gospel).

- The LFC is incarnational – that is, an extension of the incarnation. Jesus's life is a paradigm for the mission of the LFC.

---

1. Padilla, "Ecclesiology of Integral Mission."
2. Padilla, 27.
3. Padilla, 28.

- Gifts and ministries are how God equips the LFC to change society. This change reflects God's plan for creation. In effect, the community of believers is an eschatological community, bringing about the final state of God's plan for creation. This is the essence of integral mission.[4]

Padilla describes, step by step, the transforming nature of the LFC in the community. Here, he is equating the creation of resilience with integral mission. Here's how Micah Global defines integral mission:

Integral mission or holistic transformation is the proclamation and demonstration of the gospel. It is not simply that evangelism and social involvement are to be done alongside each other. Rather, in integral mission, our proclamation has social consequences as we call people to love and repentance in all areas of life. And our social involvement has evangelistic consequences as we bear witness to the transforming grace of Jesus Christ.[5]

Evangelism and social involvement have had a difficult history, but a major milestone in the reconciliation of the two took place with the Cape Town Commitment in 2011. This agreement says, in part:

Integral mission is the proclamation and demonstration of the gospel. It is not simply that evangelism and social involvement are to be done alongside each other. Rather, in integral mission, *our proclamation has social consequences as we call people to love and repentance in all areas of life.* And our social involvement has evangelistic consequences as we bear witness to the transforming grace of Jesus Christ. *If we ignore the world, we betray the Word of God*, which sends us out to serve the world. If we ignore the Word of God, we have nothing to bring to the world.

We commit ourselves to the integral and dynamic exercise of all dimensions of the mission to which God calls his Church.

God commands us to make known to all nations the truth of God's revelation and the gospel of God's saving grace through Jesus Christ, calling all people to repentance, faith, baptism, and obedient discipleship.

---

4. Padilla, 45.

5. http://www.micahnetwork.org/sites/default/files/doc/page/mn_integral_mission_declaration_en.pdf.

God commands us to reflect His character through compassionate care for the needy, and to demonstrate the values and the power of the kingdom of God in striving for justice and peace and in caring for God's creation.[6] (italics added)

Thus, integral mission is about being engaged in the community and defines how the LFC relates to those around it. As such, we find integral mission to be a defining element of the theology of resilience. There are several elements to this engagement that are also elements of resilience. We start with "our proclamation has social consequences." Integral mission is a call to awareness that our lives are created socially and have social consequences, whether we choose to recognize these or not. The implication is that impacting community resilience happens whether we specifically choose to embrace it or not. We have a choice as to whether that impact is negative or positive, but the impact is unavoidable.

The Cape Town Commitment goes on to say, "We call people to love and repentance in all areas of life." We see the reference to "all areas of life" as an emphasis on all of creation, including all people. Just as our focus is not to be narrow or only on those we prefer to see, resilience, if it is to be true resilience, must be comprehensive. Freeman and Kennedy's new book, *Indivisible: Global Leaders on Shared Security*, illustrates this holistic way of seeing the community. Their premise is that security is not found in technology or military power, nor in separating or demonizing groups of people. They argue that true security occurs when people come together to create an inclusive community with a shared concept of a common future.[7]

Conversely, "If we ignore the world, we betray God." This statement is a rejection of withdrawal and isolation. How can this betray God? Because it misrepresents God's nature, a nature revealed in our relationship to creation, a relationship of love and service. We reflect God's character when we demonstrate "compassionate care for the needy." Our relationship to the community demonstrates "the values and the power of the kingdom," values that include "justice and peace in caring for God's creation." We have already established that justice, seeking peace, and care of creation are elements of resilience. However, we must still address these questions: How does "demonstrat[ing] the values and the power of the kingdom" impact the community in a way that leads to resilience? How does the average LFC do this?

---

6. Downloaded from https://www.lausanne.org/content/ctc/ctcommitment#p1-10.

7. Freeman and Kennedy, "Indivisible."

In several of the examples and studies we shared, there is a theme of individuals and communities interpreting events and, from those interpretations, weaving an understanding of the nature of people, organizations, and communities. These shared ways of understanding are the stories people believe and discuss with one another about the character of their community and the groups that live within it. Modern society may underestimate the power and importance of these stories. Especially in the West, we emphasize evidence and documentation and too easily assume that these represent the truth that people, especially educated people, will accept. Documentation and evidence, however, are a recent phenomenon in human history. For many millennia, people created and shared their understanding of the world through stories. In these stories, people are more concerned with communicating meaning and less focused on facts. What is important in these stories is the answer to the question of *why*. Facts have a place, but it is secondary to meaning. It is meaning that is lasting and has the power to transform. Even our brains reflect this design. We store memories of what has been most meaningful to us, while events which are of secondary importance are forgotten over time. It is these meaningful events that we then form into patterns that tell us what is important about the world and the people in it. Over time, these ways of understanding permeate various aspects of our existence and, as they do so, become more established, influential, and resistant to change. Some educated people who believe in the importance of evidence (I myself [David] am an example) are mystified when people with opposing views are unimpressed by the facts. This is because it is belief and meaning that determine influence. If the evidence, especially scientific evidence, is essential to being civilized, then embrace the evidence and trust it. If the evidence is the fruit of manipulations by an educated group of elitists who are out of touch with the real world, then dismiss it as untrustworthy.

This brings us back to "demonstrat[ing] the values and the power of the kingdom." Those around us continuously interpret the meaning of our presence. That is to say, we have some impact just by existing. It is unavoidable. People see us, perhaps interact with us, and they interpret who and what we are. The more meaningful these interactions, the more likely they are to become part of the story (or worldview) other people weave about us, our relationship, and the community. The most meaningful and impactful interactions are those that involve sacrificial service to someone in need. Serving someone in need has the greatest power to influence their story and shape the meaning they assign our community (such as our faith community). Reflect on your own experience. When were you were in need and had someone help you even though they derived no benefit from doing so? It is probably a clear and meaningful memory. That experience is a demonstration of the values and power of the kingdom of God. It is the value of loving service and the power to be faithful and sacrificial in relationships and "in caring for God's creation."

Recall our discussion of the study of a major fire disaster in Sweden. The long-term impact had to do with how people interpreted the actions of various people involved in the event. Did people help one another? How timely were the responders? Did they serve everyone without prejudice? Did the government follow through on its promises? What do all of these actions, collectively, say about the nature of our community? The meaningfulness of the actions following the disaster was more influential than the disaster itself, although in different ways.

So again, how do people do this? People develop the power to do this through relationships, particularly within the faith community. The LFC is a community where people are reconciled and discipled for service. Again, Padilla puts this well:

> The church, therefore, is called to demonstrate, both in her life and in her message, this reconciliation with God and between individuals and groups. Among those who gather beneath the shadow of the cross of Christ, ethnic, social and gender divisions disappear so that "there is no longer Jew or Greek, slave or free, male or female," but "all of you are one in Christ Jesus" (Gal 3:28). The church provides a glimpse of a new humanity that in anticipation incarnates God's plan – that plan which will be brought to fruition in "the fullness of time, to gather up all things, things in heaven and things on earth in Christ" (Eph 1:10).[8]

Does sacrifice and bringing down barriers lead to resilience? A sacrificial response to those in need and bringing down barriers to relationships impact resilience in two fundamental ways: It opens up pathways to understanding, communication, and sharing of resources and – we would argue just as importantly – positively impacts the meaning people attach to community action which is essential to future resilience. In addition to community resilience, it also impacts personal resilience. When the meanings we create are constructive and help us to cope with challenges, one result is that we become more resilient. This is because beliefs that support coping are more persistent during times of stress or conflict.

---

8. Padilla, "Ecclesiology of Integral Mission," 7.

One type of action for a faith community that leads to resilient perceptions of the community is advocacy.

Resilience and a Theology of Advocacy

Padilla's theology speaks to engagement as an expression of the gospel. In this section, we summarize and excerpt a theology of advocacy using the work of Offutt et al. as a guide.[9] They begin by suggesting that evangelicals are engaged in advocacy for poverty as an individual ministry but have hesitated to engage with the power issues dimension of advocacy. Advocating for those in need to those with the power to change or maintain the structure responsible for oppression is not an area most evangelicals are comfortable with or feel prepared for. In response, Offutt and colleagues propose a theology of advocacy as a step toward equipping Christians for this task. Their model assumes the following:

- Advocacy is part of God's nature. God uses his power to confront man's needs. As such, he does so as a community of three and acts as a community on behalf of creation.
- Advocacy is evident throughout the Old and New Testaments as God deals with sin and advocates for creation. In the Old Testament, it takes several forms, including direct ultimatum, narrative, song, and wisdom.[10] In the New Testament, God not only advocates for but comes into relationship with, and alongside, creation. With the resurrection, Christ continues to advocate for us with the Father.[11]
- The Holy Spirit came so that humanity would be equipped to represent the fullness of Christ to the world. The rise of the early church became possible through the advocacy work of the Spirit.[12]

In this opening to their study, Offutt et al. position advocacy as fundamental to Scripture and God and a basic part of the Christian walk in the world. However, advocacy by Christians has lost its full meaning and power. As a solution, they describe a "transformational advocacy" directed towards powers.[13] This starts with understanding the church not as a group of

---

9. Offutt et al., *Advocating Justice*.
10. Offutt et al., 66.
11. Offutt et al., 69.
12. Offutt et al., 71.
13. Offutt et al., 80.

believers but as the body of Christ. Advocating to institutional powers is part of the work of the church as "the church exists for others in much the same way that the persons of the Trinity do."[14] In that way, Offutt and colleagues see advocacy as the work of the Spirit in the church, just as the work of the Spirit in individual believers' lives leads to the personal expression of their faith.

Moreover, quoting Lesslie Newbigin:

> We are called . . . to bring our faith into the public arena, to publish it, to put it at risk in the encounter with other faiths and ideologies in open debate and argument, and in the risky business of discovering what Christian obedience means in radically new circumstances and radically different cultures.[15]

Offutt et al. conclude by saying that local congregations are at the center of living out transformational advocacy. In sum, advocacy is part of our nature in Christ and part of our relationship with the world, just as it is at the center of God's relationship with creation. Thus, being advocates for our community is basic to living out our faith.

Resilience, Civic Engagement, and the LFC

As with social capital, the practice of LFC engagement in the community is complicated. Offutt and colleagues, writing on an evangelical vision for creating justice, note that the current practice is (in my words) out of balance. They write, "As Evangelicals, we possess robust theologies for dealing with personal sin, but limited resources for dealing with structural or institutional sin."[16] Yet, it is the role of the LFC to "speak with and on behalf of the poor, oppressed, and hungry people before those in power to name the injustices that keep people marginalized and oppressed."[17]

There have been a growing number of case studies on LFCs and civic engagement, some of which appear in a later section. For example, Burgess, studying African immigrant LFCs in the UK, describes how, as their theology moved toward becoming more holistic and community-focused, the members of these LFCs became more engaged in their community's life and quality.[18]

---

14. Offutt et al., 103.
15. Offutt et al., 103.
16. Offutt et al., 79.
17. Offutt et al., 101.
18. Burgess, "African Pentecostal Spirituality."

Theology shaped action and also informed what was possible for the LFC members.

While theology informs engagement, it can also work the other way around – and therein lies a risk. Reich and dos Santos, writing in *Latin American Politics and Society*, studied corruption in Brazil and the connection to the evangelical community. Brazil has the largest evangelical community in South America and evangelicals in Brazil tend to be active and influential in politics. The authors compared three ways in which evangelicals relate to politics: first, outright rejection of politics; second, engagement as concerned individuals only; and third, formally engaging as a function of the LFC or denomination. They then linked these three modes of engaging in known cases of corruption to see if there were any connections. In the first case, rejection of politics, there was no connection to political corruption and influence peddling. In the case of personal engagement, where political engagement is the result of personal theology and commitment and not LFC or para-LFC organizational needs and priorities, their study did not find a link with cases of corruption. In the third mode – organizational, formal, or systematic involvement in politics – they found a link to corruption, meaning that LFCs in Brazil were involved in supporting corrupt acts. This involvement resulted from the power and influence of political office impacting the values and theology of the participants. As the authors put it, "affinity with a style of machine politics . . . is particularly corruption-prone."[19] The involvement in corruption corresponded to a change in theology. In this case, the theology change was the adoption, over time, of the "prosperity gospel" and using it to justify corrupt political acts.

From these examples, we see that advocacy is not a simple matter of an LFC going out and speaking freely. The issues are complicated.

Accepting that civic engagement by the LFC is important for both the LFC and the community still leaves unanswered the question of how engaging across community barriers would make a community more resilient. We believe that work on the topic of organizational resilience contributes to understanding community resilience. Kahn et al. describe how a crisis impacts different parts of an organization differently and how these organizational units respond differently.[20] When the various parts or units work together in their response, the entire organization becomes more resilient in its response. Communities are similar. When a crisis strikes a community, it impacts different parts of

---

19. Reich and Dos Santos, "Rise (and Frequent Fall)."
20. Kahn et al., "Geography of Strain."

the community differently. Differential impact is central to the concept of social vulnerability, which was discussed previously. A fractured community is a vulnerable and less resilient community. So then, how does the process of working together take place? What determines if working together will even take place?

Kahn and his colleagues look at resilience as a process in which the various parts of an organization (or community) respond in different ways and at different times. Those closest to the point of strain or conflict are the first to be aware of a problem – for example, medical staff in an emergency room or field workers may be the first to see a disease outbreak. In our community parallel in the above paragraph, think of people closest to a flood or think of a geographic region that is the first to see the impact of climate change. Those closest may find that their resources are insufficient to respond. At this point, the people next to those closest become aware and either engage (extend resources), withdraw (disavow responsibility), or maintain the status quo (passive response). Looking at resilience as a group (or community) process allows Kahn and his colleagues to formulate resilience as a function of key group dynamics that determine which of the three responses is likely to occur. From that perspective, whether or not other units become engaged and lend resources to those closest is a function of several dynamics, including the availability of resources, the history of relations between groups, and their relative power.

Of particular interest to our discussion of resilience and the LFC is the impact of the way those who are distant from the point of impact may formulate the problem in a way that can add to the strain or damage. Distant groups either move toward or away from supporting those at the point of strain based on such factors as how they formulate responsibility and whether they see shared characteristics and shared interests. Those who move away may denigrate or blame those closest to the strain, thus justifying their reluctance to extend resources or assistance. Justice theorists describe this as blaming the victim, thus rejecting a sense of responsibility or empathy with those in need. Kahn et al. observe, "resilience is weakened when parts of a system are pathologized, ignored, distanced, withheld from or treated with indifference."[21] In contrast to blaming and pathologizing, communities build resilience when groups regularly seek shared interests and cooperation and maintain empathy.[22]

---

21. Kahn et al., 520.
22. Kahn et al., 518.

Another important dynamic, noted by several authors, is the timing of the emergency response. Timing is important in an urgent situation but different from the issue of timing in a slowly unfolding event. In an emergency, the existence of the emergency is quickly apparent. The response may be fast or slow, and delays can be perceived by the affected community as a lack of respect or concern, thus damaging community relations. In a slowly unfolding crisis such as climate change, there is the additional issue of the detection and acceptance of early signals that a crisis is developing. Those closest to the developing crisis will be the first to see changes that signal an impending disaster. Low-lying areas impacted by initial sea-level rise or areas where average temperatures are just below freezing are typical examples. The acceptance of these signals by groups distant from the vulnerable zones is more complicated, and slower compared with an urgent crisis. In 2018, when the tsunami struck Indonesia and wildfires swept through Northern California, there was no debate about whether they occurred and if they were disasters. But whether coral bleaching, drought, fire, or sea-level rise signal climate change is challenged by some who are distant from the point of impact. The challenges are complicated by the anticipated economic burden, the extent of structural changes, and other demands that may occur as climate changes. The disavowal of responsibility includes attacks on the evidence as unreliable and on those communicating the concern as misled. The disavowal risks stagnating the response and creating conflict between those who will be the first to suffer consequences and those who deny a need to extend their resources.

What role can the LFC play in such a scenario? Expanding our discussion of the nature of resilience to include group and community relationships helps reveal the important and unique role an LFC has to play. There is a well-established connection between harm and vulnerability, and often it is those who suffer the most harm who are most disadvantaged. Those with resources – and with resources comes social and political power – can more easily disavow the needs and demands of those who have less resources and thus less power. The most vulnerable among us typically do not have the power to press for attention to their needs or to exert pressure on those with more power. Alaskan natives, who are seeing their islands sink and the ice disappear, cannot compel the government to change its position on climate change. Vulnerability is a situation where the advocacy role of the LFC becomes crucial.

Similarly, advocacy is also important with regard to the issue of the timing of the response. Earlier, we described growing evidence of inequitable aid following a disaster, by both governments and aid agencies. One explanation offered is that local governments and groups drive distribution on the assumption that they know local needs. Even if this assumption has some merit, it is, at best, an imperfect guide. An LFC engaged with local vulnerable groups can be a voice for these groups and make their needs known. It is interesting to note that groups that fare better, and even profit, following a disaster are those with better education and those who are better off economically. These groups are quite likely to be capable of advocating for themselves, at least when compared with the poor and minorities. Given their greater ability to make their needs known, their influence tends to bias the assessment of needs.

Resilience, Shalom and Creation Care

Although, as far as we know, the concepts of shalom and urban shalom[23] have not been explicitly linked with resilience, we believe the theology of urban shalom is an accurate and useful contribution to the theological basis of resilience. When, as we have developed here, we see resilience as a holistic process – one based on access to resources, quality of relationships, a commitment to justice and respect for all members of the community – then shalom is a valuable way to capture this concept.

The Cape Town Commitment of 2011 reflects this holistic view of the resilient community. It links apparently diverse issues such as poverty and care of creation, and calls us to respond to destructive threats.

> Our biblical mandate in relation to God's creation is provided in *The Cape Town Confession of Faith* section 7(a). All human beings are to be stewards of the rich abundance of God's good creation. We are authorized to exercise godly dominion in using it for the sake of human welfare and needs, for example in farming, fishing, mining, energy generation, engineering, construction, trade, medicine. As we do so, we are also commanded to care for

---

23. Van Eymeren gives a good explanation of urban shalom. "The Scriptures provide us with some windows into the nature, principles and features of shalom, allowing us to apply them directly to the development of cities. Isaiah 65:17–25 is a helpful passage in this regard. Imagine living in a city where the old and young are valued for who they are and they have a clear avenue for contributing to the whole of society. This city is also a place where people's basic needs for food and shelter are met. Not by handouts but by enabling people to meet these needs themselves, thus creating a healthy reciprocity. People are also engaged in meaningful work, where work is related to personhood, dignity and the ability to meet needs, not mindless labour for disconnected corporate entities. The city also regularly celebrates its life in ways that are inclusive and promotes wellbeing. The city guided by shalom also experiences harmony between different ethnic groups, people of varying socio-economic standing and those with different levels of education" (Van Eymeren, "Creating Shalom in the City," 16).

the earth and all its creatures, because the earth belongs to God, not to us. We do this for the sake of the Lord Jesus Christ, who is the creator, owner, sustainer, redeemer, and heir of all creation.

We lament over the widespread abuse and destruction of the earth's resources, including its biodiversity. Probably the most serious and urgent challenge faced by the physical world now is the threat of climate change. This will disproportionately affect those in poorer countries, for it is there that climate extremes will be most severe and where there is little capability to adapt to them. World poverty and climate change need to be addressed together and with equal urgency.[24]

The Cape Town Commitment was followed the next year by "Creation Care and the Gospel: Jamaica Call to Action." This meeting, in Jamaica, outlined several actions for LFCs to support that target threats to our environment. The actions were based on two convictions: that creation care is part of our gospel commitment and that we face a pressing crisis that we must resolve (see appendix A). The proposed actions included a call for "action in radically reducing greenhouse gas emissions and building resilient communities," and a call

for individual Christians and the church as a whole to prophetically "speak the truth to power" through advocacy and legal action so that public policies and private practice may change to better promote the care of creation and better support devastated communities and habitats. Additionally, we call the church to "speak the peace of Christ" into communities torn apart by environmental disputes, mobilizing those who are skilled at conflict resolution, and maintaining our convictions with humility.[25]

In a similar vein, consider the WEA/Micah "Declaration on Creation Stewardship and Climate Change." Article 8 captures this holistic view of resilience, and states:

Before God we commit ourselves, and call on the whole family of faith, to bear witness to God's redemptive purpose for all creation. We will seek appropriate ways to restore and build just

---

24. https://www.lausanne.org/content/ctc/ctcommitment#p2-1-6.
25. https://www.lausanne.org/content/statement/creation-care-call-to-action.

relationships among human beings and with the rest of creation. We will strive to live sustainably, rejecting consumerism and the resulting exploitation [Matthew 6:24]. We will teach and model care of creation and integral mission. We will intercede before God for those most affected by environmental degradation and climate change, and will act with justice and mercy among, with and on behalf of them.[26]

We propose that what creation care and urban shalom are calling the LFC to respond to amounts to the creation of a resilient world. Just as proper stewardship is holistic, we are called to care for all of creation, not just parts of it; to succeed, resilience must also be holistic.

---

26. http://www.weacreationcare.org/wp-content/uploads/2014/12/micah_network_global_consultation_declaration_0.pdf.

3

Shared Resilience

We are now prepared to propose a model for resilience that incorporates the scope of the multidimensional view but with a greater emphasis on the social and communal processes that we see as foundational to resilience, which we are calling *shared resilience*. The point of using the word *shared* is that resilience requires cooperation to work toward a shared understanding of a resilient and thriving community, organization, or group. It further refers to the shared impacts of threats to resilience and to the understanding that efforts to create resilience must be broad and inclusive. Thus, the emphasis in shared resilience is at both the community and personal level, with cooperation, understanding and respect as the basis for building resilience. When parents are available and involved with their children in a way that makes them a resource for the children, then the children are more resilient and parenting takes on greater meaning for the parents. Similarly, when an LFC builds an understanding relationship with members of the community and acts as a resource for those community members, the faith experience of the faith community is richer and the community more resilient.

Engagement

In order for shared resilience to develop, community members must become engaged with their community. What do we mean by engagement? Not just being present but being in relationship with others in a way that leads to an understanding, trust, and the ability to see others' perspective. Boan et al. explored engagement across cultural boundaries in a study on preparing international development and mission workers.[1] The description of cultural

---

1. Boan et al., "Well-Prepared."

55

competence included a broad understanding and appreciation of another group's culture. Cultural competence is acquired when people take the time to interact and develop an understanding of other people. Alternatively, workers who are physically present but do not interact or learn from other people fail to acquire cultural competence.

What, then, are the community conditions that lead to engagement? Talò reviewed research on community engagement and identified seven conditions that lead to community engagement by members of the community. These are (1) a sense of community, (2) community identity, (3) social well-being, (4) place identity, (5) trust in the community, (6) trust in institutions, and (7) community cohesion.[2] In this model, engagement is broken down into seven categories, but it still leaves us with the question of *how* these characteristics come about.

Justice

As we have seen, justice has broad implications for a community. Justice is a basic dimension of shared resilience: unless justice is for everyone, it is not a just community. Most of the models we discussed either speak directly to justice or infer it.

Reducing Barriers

We have said, repeatedly, that a resilient community is one where there are few barriers to full participation in the community by all members. Shared resilience can only occur if all groups can participate in community life and resources. There are many ways that people encounter barriers to such participation: prejudice, disability, poor health, lack of financial resources, lack of skills, insecurity, poor communication, language, corruption, and more.

Some assumptions underlie our description of barriers and our recommendation that eliminating barriers is part of the mission of the church. We assert that reducing barriers is not a technical exercise but the result of building relationships, which is to say that it is the result of engagement with others. We discussed barriers under social capital. We described how LFCs build social capital but that this may either be in the service of greater barriers when it promotes in-groups or may reduce barriers when it builds capital for those with limited access. An example might help here.

---

2. Taló, "Community-Based Determinants."

In our case study of a church network in the Kakuma Refugee Camp (ch. 5), we describe how the network reduced barriers by building social structures. Elders in the network were assigned to neighborhoods (or what passes as a neighborhood in a refugee camp) and given the responsibility to listen to what was happening there, be available to hear needs and concerns, and represent those needs and concerns to the network committee. This created a voice for all people, but only because they also recognized that women and children would be underrepresented and thus required a proactive approach. Women were recruited to attend meetings and assisted in speaking out about their concerns. Children were organized into youth groups, recruited to attend youth camps, and monitored for signs of neglect or abuse. This development coupled the social capital of the neighborhood elders with a deep understanding of the barriers faced by different groups and active assistance in overcoming those barriers. The example shows how identifying, understanding, and reducing barriers to community participation requires deep local knowledge of the community and the people experiencing the barriers.

An Integrated View

We propose that shared resilience incorporates the essential evidence-based elements of the models we discussed. We summarize these models, their key elements, and the implications for the faith community in the table below. We then describe what we see as the key principles for a functioning shared resilience.

Model	Elements	Role of the Church
Trustworthy Community	Timely, appropriate (to the situation) response to those in need builds trust, shapes the perception of the community as a place to be trusted, and promotes cooperation and mutual support.	Demonstrate what it means to be a trusted community. Advocate for the disadvantaged.

Model	Elements	Role of the Church
Just Community	Justice, in all its many forms, is evident across the community and in community leadership. Like trust, it creates an expectation of fairness and promotes cooperation across groups.	Justice is central to the identity of an LFC. By being in relationship with the disadvantaged, the LFC can detect injustice and act as an advocate to the victims of injustice. This not only serves those who benefit directly but also promotes justice in the broader community.
Conservation of Resources	Suffering is directly related to the loss of resources. Thus, mitigating resource loss can lessen the impact of a crisis and promote recovery. This links to distributive and restorative justice, and trusting the community to be fair.	Life resources include faith, perception of God, and connection to the community. Thus, LFCs have both a general role in restoring lost resources – such as providing food and shelter – and a faith-specific role – such as compassionately assisting someone experiencing a crisis of faith following a traumatic loss.
Ecological Model	Resilience is best understood as based in the larger personal/community context and in how people interact with community elements. This model emphasizes the specialized knowledge people develop from being in the community, and the importance of quality engagement across the community to both develop and to make use of this community knowledge.	LFCs are most effective in advancing resilience when they see themselves as part of a larger community context.

Model	Elements	Role of the Church
Social Capital	Resilience is related to a social environment that facilitates community connections, access to social resources, and community engagement.	LFCs build social capital when they equip people for community engagement. Conversely, the LFC can detract from resilience by emphasizing community barriers and exclusiveness.
Shared Resilience Model	Shared resilience emphasizes the underlying theme in the majority of resilience models, which is a community rich in justice and social connections that foster broad participation in the community. These rich connections promote access to resources, equitable engagement, and cooperation.	The LFC models a community based on justice, engagement, and compassion, which in turn creates a reference point for community members desiring a more resilient community.

Key Principles for Creating Shared Resilience

Based on our discussion of the models of resilience, we propose that shared resilience should encompass the following principles:

Low Barriers to Access and Inclusion

The division of communities into subgroups – with little movement, communication, or resource sharing across group boundaries – impedes resilience. Recent work by Smiley et al. shows how groups tend to look inward following a disaster, focusing their restoration and social capital efforts on their own in-group, thereby creating more barriers and isolation between community groups.[3] Recognition of barriers requires a commitment to the principle that resilience only exists where it exists for everyone. Reducing barriers requires initiating and nurturing relationships across group boundaries (i.e. bridging social capital) and resisting the tendency to focus largely or exclusively on those like us. Connecting to different groups so that we can

---

3. Smiley et al., "Disasters, Local Organizations."

understand barriers from the perspective of those who live with the barriers is one strategy for countering this tendency to turn inward.

Sufficient and Available Resources

Resources are needed to buffer or absorb the impacts of loss, especially in a crisis, and to quickly restore people who have suffered loss. In addition to the resources themselves, restoration requires two things. First, the recognition that saying a resource is available – that it exists – is not meaningful unless the people who need it can also access it. Access can be limited by financial constraints, regulatory requirements, inequitable distribution, skill requirements, geographic barriers, and more. Second, recognizing the impact of vulnerability. Vulnerability to loss means that the effects of a crisis are not borne equally across a community. Depending on their vulnerability, different groups will need different types of resources. The types of vulnerability of the different groups need to be understood so that we can address variations in impact and needs. Recognizing variation is a way of saying that needs are local and varied. A broad one-size-fits-all approach will leave some groups unserved. Since it is poor and minority groups that are more likely to have special needs, the failure to accurately understand these needs ends up adding to disparities in recovery.

Commitment to Creating Justice and Building Trust

Justice is a basic requirement for community building and creating the basic conditions for resilience. Justice leads to trust and engagement, while the lack of justice leads to increased barriers, protective isolation, and low engagement. In a trusting community, the community norms prescribe trust-building behaviors that facilitate the development and maintenance of trust. For example, norms in a trusting community may prescribe that people act in trustworthy ways, speak truthfully, and come to the aid of those in need. Fukuyama, in his famous treatise on trust, argued that transaction costs plague cooperation with basic norms of trust (e.g. formalized rules and regulations, written legal contracts that require time and effort to negotiate and, at worst, to litigate). "Widespread distrust in a society, in other words, imposes a kind of tax on all forms of economic activity, a tax that high-trust societies do not have to pay."[4] By contrast, the most effective associations of people "are based

---

4. Fukuyama, *Trust*, 27–28.

on communities of shared ethical values,"[5] and the principal of those is justice. To "love mercy and act justly" is to help build social capital. Fukuyama goes on to say that building social capital

> requires habituation to the moral norms of a community and, in its context, the acquisition of virtues like loyalty, honesty, and dependability. The group, moreover, has to adopt common norms as a whole before trust can become generalized among its members. In other words, social capital cannot be acquired simply by individuals acting on their own. The acquisition requires "the prevalence of social, rather than individual virtues."[6]

Furthermore, "social capital differs from other forms of human capital insofar as it is usually created and transmitted through cultural mechanisms like religion, tradition, or historical habit."[7] The church's role in developing these individual and social virtues – chiefly justice – contributes to the community's ability to absorb, cope with, and bounce back from a variety of shocks and stresses.

Accountability and Transparency

Corruption is a worldwide threat to healthy, resilient communities. It undermines efforts to build the community characteristics described here. Transparency with social accountability is necessary to counter corruption. Open communication without fear of retribution is a value that communities must embrace and protect if transparency and accountability are to become a reality.

Restoration Following Resource Loss

We see resource losses as broad in scope and variable in importance. Once people meet their basic resource needs to maintain life (food, water, shelter, medical), additional resources for quality of life become very important. These include the need for community, social relationships, faith, security, stability, and much more (see appendix B). Restoration of the full scope of resources does not happen quickly. Sustained attention must be paid to those

---

5. Fukuyama, 26–27.

6. Fukuyama, 26–27.

7. Fukuyama, 26.

who have suffered losses to detect the long-term impact of loss and for the slow restoration of more complex resources.

Recognition of Need and Timely Response

We have seen a positive impact on the community when responses to those in need are appropriate and timely. Leaving people in need in a state of uncertainty and vulnerability increases fear and distrust. Beyond a timely response, the response must address expectations for a response. This is a matter of setting clear and accurate expectations for what the response will be before a need arises and then operating according to those expectations. For example, in the USA, people often have the unrealistic expectation that the Federal Emergency Management Agency (FEMA) will replace their home if it is destroyed by a natural disaster. This does not happen. FEMA only provides a small part of the cost of replacing a home, and this causes much anger at the government.

Engaged Local Faith Communities

We have described the various and unique contributions of LFCs to community resilience. These include filling faith needs (i.e. support for faith practices, such as worship) and faith community resource needs (i.e. support from a faith community through connectedness and spiritual support), equipping people for community engagement, shaping and improving cultural values and standards, recognizing and serving the underserved, acting as environmental stewards, building personal and community faith, and much more.

Advocacy

There will always be people groups within communities that are at a disadvantage in accessing available resources, communicating needs, and insisting on justice. Thus, there will always be a need for advocacy. Advocacy is not the unique domain of LFCs – many secular groups are doing important advocacy work – but it should be characteristic of the LFC.

Ecological Mindfulness

Finally, resilience is also about the larger environment and environmental systems. Resilience depends on the health of the environment for the simple reason that people live in and depend on the quality of the lived environment.

"Lived environment" refers to both the built environment and the natural environment. These environments are shared resources, and their condition impacts the entire community. Ecological mindfulness means being aware of our influences on the larger impacts of environmental conditions and working to maintain environments that promote health, resilience, and quality of life.

What Do We Mean by Shared?

The principles above described *working* within the community, but what do we mean by *shared* resilience? In what way is resilience shared? In describing the concept of shared resilience, we borrow from recent work by Freeman and Kennedy on shared security.[8] They see global security as arising from a sense of community and shared interest, and not from technology or military power. Shared security parallels what we are saying about resilience. Resilience does not arise from technical solutions to disasters or climate change, but from a strong and shared sense of community. In this sense, shared resilience means the following:

- Recognition that our destinies are intertwined.[9] This means that we accept that people must work together to build just and inclusive societies that recognize peace and security as rights for all people. For the LFC, this means recognizing the close link between the fate of the church and the fate of communities. As people seek peace and justice, the opportunity exists for the LFC to demonstrate the power to create justice and serve all people.
- Building a resilient society starts with empathy and compassion. Empathy can overcome the prejudices and demonization of others that is so prevalent today. We do not attain resilience if the security of one group is at the expense of another group.[10]
- The norms and values that need to change are powerful in their resistance to change. Even people who enter powerful institutions such as government often end up feeling powerless to bring about change. People must speak together to effect change. We must give a voice to the marginalized, and we must all learn to speak truth together.[11]

---

8. Freeman and Kennedy, *Indivisible.*
9. Ajlouny, "Courage to Engage."
10. Mansour, "(In)Securing Each Other."
11. Francis, "Things That Make for Peace."

- Solidarity fosters hope, and hope fosters action. Making solidarity a reality requires building bridges across communities, fostering inclusion, and countering injustice.[12]

In sum, shared resilience is the resilience that results from a community identity and purpose that includes all members of the community. It seeks justice for all community members, demonstrates empathy and compassion, restores those who have lost resources, and ensures that all share in the health of the community.

The Four Essential Practices

We suggest distilling these principles into four essential practices:

- seeking justice
- building social capital
- creating restoration
- practicing engagement

We see these practices as also essential to Christian faith and life. First, God is a God of justice. The basis of his relationship with us is justice, and he calls us to seek justice for others. By some estimates, there are 2,500 verses about justice in the Bible. For example:

> For I the LORD love justice; I hate robbery and wrongdoing. In my faithfulness I will reward my people and make an everlasting covenant with them. (Isa 61:8)

> When justice is done, it brings joy to the righteous but terror to evildoers. (Prov 21:15)

> Speak up and judge fairly; defend the rights of the poor and needy. (Prov 31:9)

Social capital is also essential; and the church represents the most basic and necessary form of social capital for our faith. The church is not an idea, it is an organism. Often – but not necessarily always – the church is also a physical structure. The church has all the elements of social capital in its roles – it brings people together for a shared purpose in worship and service, and it equips people for a life of faith. Consider some examples:

---

12. Stephan, "People Power."

> From him the whole body, joined and held together by every supporting ligament, grows and builds itself up in love, as each part does its work. (Eph 4:16)

> By the grace God has given me, I laid a foundation as a wise builder, and someone else is building on it. But each one should build with care. (1 Cor 3:10)

> For just as each of us has one body with many members, and these members do not all have the same function, so in Christ we, though many, form one body, and each member belongs to all the others. (Rom 12:4–5)

In addition to justice and social capital, our faith is also about restoration. God seeks to restore us to relationship with him and, along with us, to restore all of creation. Scripture also speaks of restoring people. For example:

> And I will bring my people Israel back from exile. They will rebuild the ruined cities and live in them. They will plant vineyards and drink their wine; they will make gardens and eat their fruit. (Amos 9:14)

> After Job had prayed for his friends, the Lord restored his fortunes and gave him twice as much as he had before. (Job 42:10)

> The poor and needy search for water, but there is none; their tongues are parched with thirst. But I the LORD will answer them; I, the God of Israel, will not forsake them. I will make rivers flow on barren heights, and springs within the valleys. I will turn the desert into pools of water, and the parched ground into springs. I will put in the desert the cedar and the acacia, the myrtle and the olive. I will set junipers in the wasteland, the fir and the cypress together, so that people may see and know, may consider and understand, that the hand of the LORD has done this, that the Holy One of Israel has created it. (Isa 41:17–20)

Finally, our faith is also about engagement. First, God did not speak to us from a distance; he descended and lived among us as we live. He engaged fully in human life. We are called to engage with the world as we respond to the call to serve those in need.

> Then the King will say to those on his right, "Come, you who are blessed by my Father; take your inheritance, the kingdom prepared for you since the creation of the world. For I was hungry and

you gave me something to eat, I was thirsty and you gave me something to drink, I was a stranger and you invited me in, I needed clothes and you clothed me, I was sick and you looked after me, I was in prison and you came to visit me."

Then the righteous will answer him, "Lord, when did we see you hungry and feed you, or thirsty and give you something to drink? When did we see you a stranger and invite you in, or needing clothes and clothe you? When did we see you sick or in prison and go to visit you?"

The King will reply, "Truly I tell you, whatever you did for one of the least of these brothers and sisters of mine, you did for me." (Matt 25:34–40)

In sum, we see the evidence for resilience as supporting a set of core practices; and these practices closely align with the role of the church in the community. When the church functions as God intended, it is both a resilient community and an agent of resilience in the community at large.

We turn now from principles to practice.

4

Application

Shared Resilience Methods and the Local Faith Community

Having described shared resilience and key principles and practices, we turn now to how to put these into action. Before discussing recommendations, it is helpful to consider actions that run counter to resilience. We have considered how an LFC's actions may fall into three categories: proactive, passive, and destructive. We described proactive actions above and will expand on this in our recommendations. We also noted that non-response or passivity sends a message that counters resilience because of how it is interpreted by the community. Some types of actions by an LFC undermine or destroy resilience. It is important to recognize both these actions and the mistaken theology that may support them. We put these negative actions into four categories: (1) increasing separation and barriers between people, (2) misuse of resources, (3) disavowing justice, and (4) confabulation or syncretism of theology with political, cultural or other schools of thought.

(1) Barriers

Barriers between people develop in a variety of ways, from an emphasis on group identity that is exclusive and rejecting of others to more aggressive methods that attack, denigrate, and demonize people. The denigration of others is characteristic of the conditions leading to attacks on minority groups and, in extreme cases, to genocide. The demonization of Jews was a prelude to the genocide in Nazi Germany, and decades of attacks on Rwandan Tutsis preceded the Rwandan genocide. While this illustrates the destructive nature of demonization when carried to extremes, demonization need not be that extreme to be harmful. Anything that makes a group appear less deserving of empathy and respect, less deserving of understanding, or less worthy to be the recipient of resources will make a community less resilient. LFCs can, perhaps inadvertently, contribute to barriers when they emphasize negative differences between the LFC and the community in ways that make community members appear less worthy of trust, justice or compassion.

(2) Resource Use

In an interesting study on the use of resources by wealthy people during an economic downturn, Betancur considered two groups of people of comparable wealth.[1] One group lived in a homogenous community of wealthy people, the other in an economically diverse community. In 2008, when the world economy declined, those who lived in the homogenous community decreased their giving and tended to hold on to their wealth, while those wealthy individuals who lived in diverse communities increased their giving. The explanation was that the homogenous communities were characterized by exclusiveness – as illustrated by walled and gated communities – while those living in diverse communities had relationships with people who were relatively less wealthy and were experiencing more hardships. The second group's connection with a diverse community increased their empathy for others' hardships, and they responded with compassion and a greater willingness to give.

(3) Disavowing Justice

The disavowal of justice occurs when people in need are not seen as having a just need. One way we do this is by faulting people for their circumstances, also called blaming the victim. Saying that a need or problem is the fault of the person in need removes any pressure we may feel to do something to help. Blaming is arguably one of the greatest barriers to humanitarian action and justice. It is seen in ideas such as these: poor people need to get a job; sick people need to clean up their lifestyle; people in developing countries have just become dependent on aid. These are simply rationalizations that excuse our inaction. Matthew 26:6–13 provides an example of using theology to excuse just action:

> While Jesus was in Bethany in the home of Simon the Leper,
> a woman came to him with an alabaster jar of very expensive

---

1. J. Betancur, "Gentrification and Community," 383–406.

perfume, which she poured on his head as he was reclining at the table.

When the disciples saw this, they were indignant. "Why this waste?" they asked. "This perfume could have been sold at a high price and the money given to the poor."

Aware of this, Jesus said to them, "Why are you bothering this woman? She has done a beautiful thing to me. The poor you will always have with you, but you will not always have me. When she poured this perfume on my body, she did it to prepare me for burial. Truly I tell you, wherever this gospel is preached throughout the world, what she has done will also be told, in memory of her."

A common interpretation of this passage is that Jesus is saying caring for the poor is not important because there will always be poor people. Therefore, trying to eliminate poverty is pointless. That interpretation is at odds with other Scriptures, including the Old Testament passage Jesus was referencing:

If anyone is poor among your fellow Israelites in any of the towns of the land the LORD your God is giving you, do not be hardhearted or tightfisted toward them. Rather, be openhanded and freely lend them whatever they need. Be careful not to harbor this wicked thought: "The seventh year, the year for canceling debts, is near," so that you do not show ill will toward the needy among your fellow Israelites and give them nothing. They may then appeal to the LORD against you, and you will be found guilty of sin. Give generously to them and do so without a grudging heart; then because of this the LORD your God will bless you in all your work and in everything you put your hand to. There will always be poor people in the land. Therefore I command you to be openhanded toward your fellow Israelites who are poor and needy in your land. (Deut 15:7–11)

Why, then, does this common interpretation, that Jesus is discounting the value of caring for the poor, persist? There are two reasons. The first, mentioned above, is that it eliminates the tension we feel when we see someone in need, especially if their condition is far worse than our own in terms of health, wealth, or security. The second reason goes back to what we have said earlier about attaching meaning to our experiences. Once such interpretations are made, and especially when these are supported by those around us, they can develop into a persistent meaning we attach to poverty. When this happens, we become less likely to see poor people as individuals in their own right and tend to view them as members of a group of people who are not truly deserving of justice or of our compassionate response.

(4) Syncretism

Syncretism is the amalgamation or blending of different views, religions, cultures, or schools of thought. Speaking at the 2015 Micah Triennial, Joseph Nyamutera addressed the issue of how Rwanda, a country where 90 percent of the people claim to be Christian, could become the site for one of the worst genocides in history.[2] One description of the root causes was the confabulation of Christian faith with cultural bias and myth about the nature and origin of different tribes. This syncretism of faith and myth contributed to the devaluing and demonizing of the Tutsi tribe, eventually leading to the easy denial of humanity and justification of violence.

Today, many countries are facing the rise of nationalism and, along with it, religious nationalism, which is a type of syncretism. Nationalism is the emphasis on the needs, rights, and values of one's nation to the exclusion of other nations. Because it elevates those associated with national identity above other groups, it is often the source of racism and other forms of bias and hatred.

We offer a notorious example of syncretism in Westboro Baptist Church (WBC) in Kansas. This church gained international attention after it picketed the funerals of American soldiers killed after 9/11 and the war in Afghanistan. The church leader, Fred Phelps, claimed that these soldiers died because the military accepted homosexuals and God hates homosexuals. Indeed, he went further, teaching that God hated all people who did not conform with his – that is, Phelps's – political and religious views. Researcher Rebecca Barrett-Fox linked the syncretistic views of WBC to the larger religious right movement in the USA, showing how political and religious views were increasingly confabulated, leading to the elevation of the rights and values of certain people – for example, straight military personnel – over the rights and needs of others.[3] WBC is an extreme example of a trend in the larger religious right movement where politics embraces conservative religion when it advances political interests and, in turn, conservative theology is adjusted to align with political and nationalistic views. Today, other examples can be found in statements from religious leaders supporting the exclusion of immigrants with

2. J. Nyamutera, "Truth and Reconciliation."
3. Barrett-Fox, *God Hates.*

pronouncements that heaven will have a wall around it and so building a border wall is biblical[4] or claiming that limiting immigration from Muslim countries is necessary for security reasons.[5] There have also been pronouncements critical of government decisions, such as the criticism of the US government separating children from their parents at the US southern border.[6]

The critical concern is when confabulation of faith and politics not only distorts faith teachings but also supports barriers between people, which leads, eventually, to the denial of compassion and justice to some groups of people.

The Resilience-Enhancing LFC

There are many recommended actions for LFCs proposed by those working in development, creation care, urban shalom, and other movements. We see these actions as holistic community movements that build community resilience. Rather than aggregating all these various proposals, we list what we see as the basic or core actions by LFCs that will strengthen the community. We start with a general description of basic actions and go on to specific recommendations for action.

Seeking Justice

Resilience has a strong connection to lower barriers between groups within a community, equal participation, and active open communication. In fact, there is a growing and substantial body of research on the socioeconomic importance of social capital in helping to build social cohesion across the various groups within a community for more effective information and resource sharing during times of stress.[7] (We discussed this at length in previous sections.) The links to all forms of justice are apparent. Justice and resilience are both served

---

4. https://www.huffingtonpost.com/entry/preacher-robert-jeffress-border-wall-trump_us_5c3640d2e4b00c33ab5f394b.

5. https://www.vox.com/2018/10/30/18035336/white-evangelicals-immigration-nationalism-christianity-refugee-honduras-migrant.

6. https://www.vox.com/2018/6/18/17475892/white-house-migrant-families-biblical-franklin-graham-sbc-catholic-bishops.

7. Adger, "Social Capital"; Aldrich, *Building Resilience*; Baron, Field, and Schuller, *Social Capital: Critical Perspectives*; Bebbington, "Sharp Knives"; Bourdieu, "Forms of Capital"; Chambers and Kopstein, "Bad Civil Society"; Putnam, *Making Democracy Work*; Putnam, *Bowling Alone*; Szreter, "State of Social Capital"; Szreter and Woolcock, "Health by Association?"; Tatsuki and Hayashi, "Seven Critical Element Model," 1–20; Woolcock, "Social Capital and Economic Development"; Woolcock, "Social Capital in Theory."

when all people are equally able to access resources and participate in society, when those who are less capable are supported, and the actions by society and political groups are subject to open dialogue.

Aldrich's influential work on the role of social capital in resilience highlighted the differences between bonding, bridging, and linking social capital. LFCs offer the opportunity for like individuals to coalesce around a shared identity and offer that bonded group the opportunity for more effective collective action. Given the right spiritual leadership and encouragement, that tightly bonded group can leverage resources accessed from its vertical linkages with more powerful, authoritative, and resource-rich networks to benefit other groups within the community. In order to do this effectively, however, the LFC must be bridged well enough with other vulnerable groups within the community to empathize with them, realize their unique needs, and understand how best to contribute to the resilience of those groups. One obvious way is through seeking justice for marginalized, overlooked, neglected, or oppressed groups within the community.

The book of Jeremiah cites a letter from the prophet Jeremiah to the Jewish exiles, priests, prophets, and "all the other people Nebuchadnezzar had carried into exile from Jerusalem to Babylon." The Lord commands them to "seek the peace and prosperity of the city to which I have carried you into exile."[8] While this is a specific exhortation to the Jewish exiles in Babylon, several sociological truths and relationships are found in this rich Scripture. God's command to the Jews extended far beyond caring for their own needs or even caring for the basic needs of those around them. It included intermarriage – typically a powerful and effective way to bridge between tightly bonded groups and get to know other cultures and norms intimately – and the wisdom that "if it [city] prospers, you too will prosper."[9] This wisdom of God, communicated through the prophet, highlights a key aspect of community resilience: one's individual ability to cope with and recover from shocks or stresses, no matter how minor, is directly linked to the community's well-being and reveals the importance of bridging social capital for resource sharing and advocating for justice.

The LFC, through vertical linkages with higher levels of religious affiliation and horizontal linkages with LFCs in other parts of the world, can wield significant influence when properly leveraged, not least in contexts where governmental authorities are sympathetic to Christianity. In this sense, the LFC constitutes a highly visible platform for seeking justice and loving mercy

---

8. Jer 29:2, 7.
9. Jer 29:7.

(Mic 6:8). With religions and religious leaders increasing in prominence and influence among developing communities worldwide,[10] LFCs "are increasingly seen in development studies as important generators of social capital through building networks between people and fostering trust relationships between their members."[11]

We acknowledge that, in many communities, the local Christian church is often one of the marginalized, excluded, and sometimes even oppressed, groups within a community, which require justice. The same related concepts of social capital and justice apply. Martin Luther King Jr., in his *Letter from Birmingham Jail*, wrote, "Injustice anywhere is a threat to justice everywhere. We are caught in an inescapable network of mutuality, tied in a single garment of destiny. Whatever affects one directly, affects all indirectly."[12] In order to pursue justice for others as well as for itself, the LFC must be aware of the pitfalls of selective reciprocity, particularistic separatism, divisiveness, and exclusion that so easily result when LFCs are so inward-looking and tightly bonded that bridging relationships outside the group becomes unlikely.[13] This is true both when the LFC is seeking justice for others and when seeking justice for itself. When seeking justice for itself, the LFC will often require the support and empathies of other, sometimes more powerful, groups for advocacy, voice, and representation. Again, a healthy LFC is a powerful driver of community well-being and resilience.

Building Social Capital

According to Ayers, in a study of the role of LFCs in building resilience to cyclones in the Ayeyarwady River Delta region of Myanmar, the ways in which LFCs "optimize social capital" or balance the positive and negative contributions of LFCs to social capital is critical.[14] As discussed elsewhere in the book, LFCs can be powerful agents of change in their communities, but their effectiveness for positive change depends, in large part, upon the spiritual health of the faith community itself. "LFCs range 'from being a balm for the body and soul to being a divisive force in a community'. . . 'The question is

---

10. Haynes, *Religion and Development*; Deneulin and Bano, *Religion in Development*; Sen, *Development as Freedom*; Narayan, *Voices of the Poor*; Fiddian-Qasmiyeh and Ager, "Local Faith Communities."

11. Deneulin and Bano, *Religion in Development*, 48–49.

12. M. L. King Jr., *Letter from Birmingham Jail*.

13. Chambers and Kopstein, "Bad Civil Society."

14. Ayers, "Social Capital, Resilience," 47.

about whether their [LFC's] stated values, beliefs, creed, agenda, ideology, or platform is clearly incompatible with a belief in equal moral consideration' and how those are presented and reinforced by church leadership."[15] In order to optimize social capital, Ayers recommends that LFCs and their leaders should "seek to be inclusive and public-regarding of other LFC[s]" and lists the following recommendations for doing so:

- Care for the needs of *all* elderly, sick, or needy, regardless of religious affiliation.
- Encourage reciprocal donations between LFCs.
- Share resources with other LFCs, where possible.
- Seek to include other LFCs in festivals and events. Encourage reciprocation.
- Network/connect with outside sources of help and be equitable in resource distribution to all LFCs in the community, especially in disaster recovery phases.
- Strategize with religious leaders and village elders for a community-wide vision.
- Where possible, encourage cooperation and collaboration between those with different livelihoods.[16]

Practicing Engagement

The above recommendations on social capital lead to the need for engagement. Note the language used of care for others, sharing, including, cooperating, or collaborating. These are all forms of engagement. When a house of worship creates ways for people to participate in the life of that house of worship, it prepares people for engagement. The skills learned by participating in an internal group can be built upon to prepare people to participate in community-based services and events. Participation by serving, teaching, worship, or speaking are starting points for increased engagement that can lead to more community focused actions.

Engagement brings down barriers by promoting understanding. It also counters the tendency to only speak with those who share our views and thus have our biases reinforced. Interacting exclusively with people who share our views has the effect of moving people toward more extreme and

---

15. Ayers, 60.
16. Ayers, 61.

excluding views. This isolating tendency is in full display in social media, where people can easily focus on groups that share and reinforce. These social media interactions emphasize differences between people as part of defining themselves. In time, these differences become barriers as people are increasingly uncomfortable with interacting with people of different views. The antidote to this is real-world relationship building and engagement. It is only by having a real-world (as opposed to online) social experience that people grow in their understanding and respect for others. LFCs can create opportunities for these contacts by building social capital that assists people in engaging with others.

Creating Restoration

Consistent with the evidence on resource loss, restoration is essential for mitigating harm and promoting recovery. As we discussed, restoration needs to be considered broadly, including the social, material, physical, and spiritual aspects of restoration. Restoration builds on the first two elements of justice and capital. Restoration must reflect justice by being fair and equitable, timely, and in proportion to loss. The restoration that reflects justice builds upon engagement that informs the LFC about community needs, and social capital that provides ways to connect and communicate. Another example may help. In many communities, emergency services recognize that there are vulnerable groups – that are at great risk in certain emergencies –which emergency responders find difficult to locate so that they can be protected. In some settings, LFCs were recruited to help emergency responders locate and assist vulnerable groups. The LFCs were most often engaged with these groups, knew how to find them in a crisis, and understood some of the issues and barriers to protecting and caring for them in a crisis. Working with emergency responders mitigated some of the dangers faced by marginalized groups during a crisis and directed subsequent services toward those in need.

Action Recommendations for the LFC

In this section, we bring together the actions presented or suggested previously, grouped according to different aims or issues. Rather than list a set of ideal actions, we approach this by thinking about how capacity develops over time. We start by assuming this is entirely new to the reader and describing how to introduce a new mission concept to an LFC and gain their support. We then move through different scenarios and offer suggestions for how LFCs with established missions could enhance their contribution to community resilience.

Getting the LFC House in Order

Since having an impact is about who you are as well as what you do, a frank self-assessment is good place to start. In teaching resilience, we emphasize that serving justice begins with the church being a window into a community of justice. When people in the community around you look at your faith community, do they see a community that is above reproach?

Managing finances "creatively" is sometimes seen as fair practice, especially when supporters are wealthy and the urgent need for funds is used to justify questionable practices. In a community that had recently suffered a natural disaster, a foundation provided money to a local church network to have a retreat where they could organize and plan their approach to rebuilding. As the participants were leaving, the organizer went to the hotel clerk to pay for his room. The clerk asked, "What would you like me to put on the receipt?" Puzzled, the organizer asked, "What do you mean?" The clerk explained that the other participants had asked that a larger amount be shown on the receipt so they would be reimbursed an additional amount. Shocked, the organizer called an urgent meeting to discuss integrity and have the finances corrected.

Besides being a just community above reproach, having a community impact also depends on demonstrating respect for others, especially those who are different from the majority. This is our view on what it means to show humility, as in Micah 6:8 which calls for justice, mercy, and humility. Humility is not just avoiding self-exaltation; it also requires respect for others. Thinking little either of yourself or of others is not humility – because humility is grounded in respect for both self and others. Showing respect and humility sets the stage for a trusting relationship. Like love, humility and respect do not mean we approve of everything another person does. It does mean we have an unwavering respect for others as part of God's creation even while we may struggle with certain behaviors.

Taking the issue of humility a step further, respecting others can be a challenge when we have suffered an injustice. In chronic conflict areas, we have observed that parents, community leaders, and even faith leaders may teach vengeance to their children in the hope that, as they grow, they will attain justice for the community. Such teaching perpetuates violence and is one of the reasons chronic conflicts are so difficult to change.

With the LFC house in order, the next step may be to introduce a new ministry.

When introducing a new mission or ministry concept:

In some cases, the leadership of the LFC may have a vision for the LFC and how it engages the community, and now they need to engage the membership to make that vision a reality. The identity of the LFC, including its mission and how it relates to the larger world, are all parts of a model people carry in their minds. That model is created, maintained, and changed through conversation. Therefore, the task involved in introducing a new mission or strengthening an existing mission is to change the conversations among members. Doing this involves several tasks, all of which are fairly straightforward:

- Decide on the message.
- Make sure there is a consistent message from leadership.
- If there are several people on the staff, work to create a consistent message among all staff.

When ensuring that the work with the community does not detract from the community's resilience:

- Recognize the signs that the LFC might act in ways that counter the resilience of the community.
- Consider your relationship with other faith groups.
- Confront signs of blaming the victim or demonizing minority groups (discussed under justice).

When preparing or building capacity for the LFC to engage in community ministry:

- Start with theology. This is essential for linking faith and action, and ensuring that the work is an expression of the LFC's mission.
- Develop a theology of mission and community service.
- Create opportunities for members to participate in the community at multiple levels –within the LFC, within the community at large, and internationally.
- Identify and teach the skills of engagement which are important when assisting those in need.

When engaging in a partnership or coalition to serve the community:

Forming community partnerships that include LFCs is increasingly popular. The challenge for the LFC is to be prepared to be a strong partner and not simply an extension of the other organization. Working in a partnership where the LFC plays a clear and unique role can be a way to engage members in ministry and demonstrate the work of the LFC. Without a clear mission and role, the LFC can appear to have nothing unique to offer. This can give the impression that other "experts," rather than the LFC, do the important work of building the community. Some have referred to this as the "institutionalization of mercy." The practice of mercy has become another technical skill, requiring that organizations be staffed with technical experts. LFCs need to be alert to this risk, starting by asking themselves how they demonstrate mercy to the community in a way that is distinct from the technical work of others.

- Have a clear purpose and role in the coalition that is connected to the LFC's mission.
- Develop and communicate the theological and scriptural basis for that role.
- Communicate the role to all members of the coalition.
- When a partnership acquires ministry resources, take care to separate the long term and sustaining resources of the LFC from short term program resources. If possible, form a separate entity to receive and manage those resources, so that the core resources of the LFC remain untouched.

When considering a culture change within the local community:
Culture change can seem to be one of those abstract, technical skill areas beyond the reach of an LFC. In practice, LFCs are often the center for maintaining and communicating culture. Let us start by demystifying culture change. We create, maintain, and change culture through social interactions among people who trust one another. When a faith leader speaks, when faith community members discuss what the faith leader says, and when we integrate those teachings into other aspects of our lives, culture is embedded within us.

In the same way, we can change a culture. Consider the story in chapter 5 about early child marriage in Cameroon. Cultural support for early marriage was changed by the LFC through a systematic effort to teach, engage, and discuss the issue of early marriage. It was not quick, but it was effective.

When a cultural issue results in sustaining an injustice, the LFC has a powerful role to play in changing that cultural issue.

When preparing to play a part in disaster response or crisis:
If the LFC disaster response involves joining a cooperative effort, then the issues discussed above under partnering apply here as well. But what about the specific ministries that an LFC can offer?

It is easier to create or develop services for disaster response than to maintain them, especially in areas where disasters are infrequent. It is challenging to retain volunteers for something unpredictable and infrequent because they start losing their skills as well as losing interest. There are several alternatives.

One alternative to a disaster response ministry is to look at the existing ministries of the LFC and ask how they might adapt, expand, or pivot (from ongoing ministry to disaster response) when a crisis occurs. When people are displaced by a disaster, a ministry of feeding the homeless might be scaled up and even work in partnership with other homeless ministries. The continual ministry of care for the homeless creates a core of volunteers who acquire and maintain critical crisis skills. Rotating other LFC members through this ministry gives people experience that prepares them to join an expanded effort in response to a crisis.

Another alternative is to focus on reducing disaster risk. A detailed discussion of risk reduction is beyond the scope of this book, but we will mention a few important points. As we have repeatedly emphasized, disasters fall most heavily on the vulnerable. Further, we trace the causes of vulnerability to injustice. Thus, we argue that a ministry to reduce vulnerability by confronting injustice is exactly the type of ministry that would be conducted by a just community. Further, a ministry to reduce vulnerability builds community relationships and improves the conditions that make a community more resilient in addition to having less risk exposure. We list some resources for risk reduction in appendix C.

When preparing to play a part in a slowly unfolding disaster:

We use the term "slow disasters" in order to correct the idea that all disasters are crises. Climate change is a slowly unfolding disaster. So is the reduction in basic services that protect people – for example, child immunizations, quality education, and reduction in access to food and shelter. Relief and development in response to slow disasters is similar to work in risk reduction. Because it is a slow change, an assessment of the change and identification of impacted people is very important. For example, while Rwanda is not a country generally known for its disasters, the severity and frequency of disasters are increasing as a result of climate change. Rwanda is a mountainous country that is seeing a change in rainfall patterns. Rain is now coming in more concentrated periods, resulting in increased flooding. The changing rain patterns expose people who live in downstream drainage areas to much greater flood risk. In this situation, the Rwandan LFCs may do the following:

- Map out the risks. What areas are prone to flooding and who lives there? How has the risk changed, and is there an identifiable pattern? A common error is to assume that what happened during the past ten years will be the pattern for the next ten. But it is important to see a pattern to help us to understand where and how the risk is growing.
- Map out resources. Who is helped, and who is helping? Are there gaps in this aid?
- What do the local people think is the best solution? Often the people who live with the problem have the greatest insight into what to do about it. If the LFC is forming a team, make local people part of the team. If the LFC is doing an assessment, bring in local people to help review and interpret the assessment.
- Strategize and implement the approach.

Our aim here is not to teach risk reduction or disaster response but to introduce these topics as a way to show that they are within reach of the LFC and consistent with a faith community's service to the local community.

Action Recommendations for Faith Networks and Associations

For several years now, I (David) have had the honor of working with the World Evangelical Alliance (WEA) on humanitarian advocacy. The WEA philosophy of church development emphasizes the role of the Alliance as responding to concerns that arise from the grassroots of the organization. The basis for this view is partly a concern that the alternative is a top-down approach that can come across as being imposed upon the local community. This is certainly an important concern for a global organization. It assumes that the initiatives that arise from within the local church are those that will be most important to, and most engaging of, the membership. Thus, the global organization's role is to listen and be responsive.

I am mostly in agreement with this view. In my case, I generally only visit communities or work with organizations where I have been invited. But this view, like any other, requires a balancing perspective. Local communities often need input as to the possibilities for mission and service. This is especially true in regions where educational resources and communications are limited. As I write, for example, meetings have taken place with local faith leaders in Cameroon regarding the continuing violence and the rapidly increasing numbers of displaced people. The meetings are partly discussion and partly educational. Micah and WEA initiated meetings as faith leaders expressed growing concern about the numbers of displaced people and the ongoing suffering. There was a concern, but there was also uncertainty about what a LFC could do, should do, and should be capable of doing. The meetings provided examples and theological framing for local faith community service to the displaced, followed by discussion and shared decision making, which led to requests for more organizing and educational help. This example illustrates how national and global leadership can facilitate the process of local mission development without violating the emphasis on grassroots initiatives.

As a US-trained psychologist, I am reminded how, until the late 1960s, physical child abuse was seldom reported in the USA. Physicians who treated children with physical injuries – that today we know are evidence of abuse – were unable to consider that parents might be the ones to inflict such injuries. Then, in the mid-1950s, a Denver hospital created multidisciplinary teams between pediatricians and social workers. The social workers had the training and, importantly, the language to see and discuss parental child abuse. Once the hospital implemented these teams, the identification and intervention into child abuse took off.[17] Organizational psychologist Karl Weick describes this as an example of the connection between an organization's ability to see and discuss something and its ability to also see a possible course of action. Weick describes the "life trailing" nature of experience and understanding that makes adapting to a new reality very difficult.[18] Engaging with people who can introduce new concepts and language, and link these to faith, is critical for a group to find the energy to act and the hopefulness that they can do something meaningful. With this in mind, we suggest the following for faith alliances:

- Prioritize for action the alliances and church networks in areas facing major disruptions and threats, such as frequent natural disasters (e.g. Philippines, Bangladesh), chronic conflict (e.g. Venezuela, South Sudan, Congo, Cameroon), or rapid climate change (e.g. South Pacific, West Africa). Actions would include close monitoring, engaging local groups in a discussion of impacts, needs and desired response, and equipping national networks with strategies for engaging with global resources and fostering resilience.
- Conduct a campaign to educate associations representing INGOs about the contributions of LFCs. As part of the campaign, assess

---

17. Weick, "Faith, Evidence, and Action."
18. Weick, 3.

local impact partnerships for disaster response to identify useful lessons and strategies.

- Develop and disseminate resources on a theology of community engagement and resilience.

Action Recommendations for NGOs
How implications for NGOs differ from implications for LFCs

Non-governmental organizations (NGOs), whether local or international, faith-based or secular, are unique entities, apart from LFCs in many respects. First, NGO mandates can be as multisectoral as to include nearly every aspect of human flourishing or as narrow and focused as livestock health or tree planting. These mandates can be derived and rooted in faith-based perspectives or tied to secular humanist ideologies or rights-based approaches. Furthermore, NGO stakeholders, both internal and external to the organization (i.e. staff, donors, advocates, or partners), wield significant influence and, in some cases, lay claim to the organizational objectives, policies, and practices in ways that are typically significantly different from the LFC. Moreover, by operating alongside secular agencies in a highly secularized relief and development industry, NGOs are sometimes signatories to various codes of conduct and commitments to industry best practices, both out of a commitment to the highest quality work possible and to appeal to donors who prioritize quality and effectiveness. As such, staff at NGOs may be highly specialized technical professionals with expertise in narrow, well-defined fields like health, nutrition, food security, or logistics. All these factors influence how an NGO views the world in which it works and how it interacts with relief and development stakeholders, including LFCs. Consider what may happen when an NGO encounters an LFC with very clear ideologies and perspectives that are historically rooted in ancient tradition and experience, with clearly defined and unalterable – albeit holistic and comprehensive – mandates, with a typically homogenous internal stakeholdership (ideologically-speaking), often under a single leader, and with an ultimate, spiritual external stakeholder. The NGO may find it difficult to understand how best to engage with the LFC in healthy and effective ways that are mutually beneficial and that recognize the sovereignty and particular mandates of both agencies. A few of the most common difficulties, cited elsewhere in this book, are the relative resource imbalances (financial and otherwise) that NGOs introduce – that can lead to improper influence and power differentials – and the often utilitarian approach of NGOs with LFCs viewed as simple functionaries or operational extensions of the NGO's expressed intentions in the community.[19] As such, recommendations for LFCs engaging with NGOs are sometimes protective. In light of all of this, we put forward a few conservative recommendations for how NGOs can best engage with LFCs for building community resilience.

Work on sustainability and resilience suggests that there are important interactions between the two. Hou and colleagues describe research showing how people are more resilient, even when faced with ongoing violence, when they can maintain daily activities and access resources. This shows "the importance of building a resource-endowed environment that is conducive to resilience."[20] Recall our discussion earlier, that resources do not necessarily mean material resources; social, human, spiritual, political, and even natural resources are also critical in everyday living.

Furthermore, how these resources are utilized and combined directly impacts the value of these resources for recovering from the myriad challenges, shocks, and stresses that face vulnerable communities around the world. Thus, in our view, a "resource-endowed environment" (to use Hou's term) would be a community environment that not only has resources but creates and sustains access to those resources for all members of the community. Access to these resources creates satisfaction and meaning in life and promotes resilience when individuals and communities experience a crisis. Thus, sustaining the community group processes that create cooperation, timely response in times of need, and resource sharing (to name a few key characteristics) lead to a more resilient community. They are sustained when they are characteristics of the daily community and personal lives of the community members – that is to say, they are enduring characteristics embedded in the life and culture of the community rather than reactive or temporary features that appear only in time of need. Because they are embedded and enduring, they create resilience daily as well as during times of extreme events. Sustained characteristics lead to resilience and resilience, in turn, sustains the community and its members.

From the NGO perspective, the challenge is how to access and contribute to those key and sustaining characteristics. The need to engage communities and enhance resilience has been understood for some time but, according to Imperiale and Vanclay, practice has a long way to go before it catches up with theory.[21] They describe the international community response to disasters, and to the reconstruction and development that follows, as still

---

19. Burchardt, "Faith-Based Humanitarianism."
20. Hou et al., "Measuring Everyday Processes," 716.
21. Imperiale and Vanclay, "Experiencing Local Community Resilience."

failing to understand and embrace local resilience capabilities and processes. Instead, they see a persistent reliance on command and control "deployed by disaster management agencies [that] results in increasing dependency on external support and annihilates the potentialities of local communities."[22] They challenge NGOs to learn to recognize underlying community-at-large resilience so they can work in concert with those capabilities and develop more sustainable responses that build on the strengths of the entire community.

To this end, we make the following recommendations for NGOs working in communities with an LFC.

(1) Embrace political and social capital and the LFC's role in them.

"Scholars and practitioners have increasingly recognized that development is a fundamentally political process, and there are concerted efforts underway to develop more politically-informed ways of thinking and working."[23] In order to move the conversation beyond the project-level concerns around sustainability (i.e. will the outcomes and services achieved by the project continue beyond the funded period) to a fuller understanding of sustainability in terms of "sustainable poverty escapes" (i.e. if we help households and communities escape poverty – regardless of how we define "poverty" – is that escape sustainable long after we exit?), the NGO community must embrace the power and complexities of political and social capital.[24]

In a review of programs claiming to think and work politically (TWP),[25] Laws and Marquette reveal seven recurring success factors: (1) "politically smart" programs that are (2) "locally-led," utilizing (3) "iterative problem-solving," (4) "brokering relationships," (5) "flexibility," (6) and long-term commitments in (7) a "supportive environment."[26] These success factors are facilitated by political economy analysis (PEA)[27] performed early on in the community development process. "PEA is a structured approach to examining power dynamics and economic and social forces that influence development."[28]

---

22. Imperiale and Vanclay, 204.

23. Laws and Marquette, "Thinking and Working Politically," Executive Summary.

24. Shepherd et al., *Chronic Poverty Report*.

25. https://twpcommunity.org/.

26. Laws and Marquette, "Thinking and Working Politically," 8.

27. For a detailed explanation of PEA and TWP, refer to USAID's Guide for Practitioners: https://usaidlearninglab.org/sites/default/files/resource/files/pea_guide_final.pdf.

28. Menocal et al., "Thinking and Working Politically," 1.

At a minimum, this entails including social capital assessment and analysis in appraisal methodology for programming, specifically focused on the roles of LFCs and religious leaders in the socioeconomic fabric of the target community. More comprehensively, it should include the LFC as a recognized institution with its own power dynamics, incentives, and local knowledge in more "iterative cycles of planning, action, reflection, revision" and a recognition of the LFC's value for "facilitating, convening and brokering partnerships and spaces for collective action based on long-term engagement, with focus on local ownership."[29] Furthermore, NGOs can support and contribute to the remit of LFCs by providing leadership training to religious leaders, helping LFCs engage more effectively in conflict-resolution programs, and providing space for interfaith dialogue.

(2) Create space for LFCs to engage with the broader relief and development community on their own terms.

There is increasing recognition of local faith communities as important partners in development. We have presented a variety of evidence to support this view and to detail how LFCs contribute to community resilience. Ager et al. clearly described the importance of such partnerships.[30] However, as we note, the nature of the partnership is a critical part of realizing the potential for such an arrangement. The World Evangelical Alliance (WEA), in response to a call for contributions to the World Humanitarian Summit of 2016 from the faith-based community, developed *A Call to Commitment and Partnership: A World Evangelical Alliance Brief on the Evangelical Community and Humanitarian Development*. WEA's brief makes this recommendation: "Recognizing there are multiple groups among civil society, create a permanent space for the faith community to participate at the strategic planning level by, for example, encouraging UNOCHA [United Nations Office for the Coordination of Humanitarian Affairs]to formally acknowledge/engage the faith community in disaster planning and response."[31]

Rather than taking the typical utilitarian view of LFCs as tools to be used in the achievement of NGO objectives, we recommend that NGOs take a less interventionist approach and adopt a more *brokering* approach through the creation of space for LFCs to engage with the broader relief and development

---

29. Menocal et al., 3.

30. Ager, Fiddian-Qasmiyeh, and Ager, "Local Faith Communities."

31. World Evangelical Alliance, "Call to Commitment," 23.

community as power brokers themselves, on their own terms. Part of this NGO role will inevitably include translation of the LFCs' perspectives, understandings, needs, and requirements to a highly secular, highly technical industry, as well as the protection of that space "at the table" with more traditional social and political groups. Various faith-based NGOs – including Tearfund,[32] World Relief,[33] and Food for the Hungry[34] – have developed church leader training curricula that help develop these brokerage capacities for churches. While there may be growing recognition of LFCs and religious leaders as important players in community development and relief, secular actors remain more comfortable and well-versed in dealing with secular institutions, agencies, and civil society organizations and may, therefore, be inclined to continue overlooking or excluding LFCs and religious leaders.

(3) Advocate for the rightful place and role of LFCs at higher levels of humanitarian policy

While faith-based NGOs may better understand the unique nature of LFCs and how best to engage with them regularly, secular NGOs and agencies often remain uninformed.

NGOs should strive to engage in more equitable partnerships with LFCs, partnerships that leverage true comparative advantages in order to continue developing an empirical evidence base that highlights the unique value of LFCs, and thus to enhance recognition and acceptance of LFCs as critical and effective local agents of change. This empirical evidence base will be vital in continuing to influence higher-level stakeholders of the international community – for example, the World Bank, UN agencies, governments, and other intergovernmental agencies. The NGO's unique ability to understand the language and remit of the LFC, and to translate between the LFC and these higher-level relief and development actors, is key to more progress on sustainable poverty escapes for the world's most vulnerable people.

---

32. https://learn.tearfund.org/en/themes/disasters/disasters_and_the_local_church/.

33. https://worldrelief.org/church-leaders-toolkit/.

34. Church Leaders Training Manual available upon request from Josh Ayers (jayers@fh.org).

5

Stories of Shared Resilience

An Example from Kenya: A Refugee Church Network in Kakuma, Kenya 2014[1]

In 1997 a refugee pastor formed an association of churches from among the churches in the Kakuma Refugee Camp in Kenya. Known as the United Refugee Churches (URC), it helped promote cooperation and eliminate conflict between the churches in and around the Kakuma Camp in Kenya. At that time, the camp environment was characterized by frequent conflict between tribes and denominations. If one group received an outside donation, it set off a conflict between groups. The underlying problems were distrust and a strong sense of injustice that would quickly trigger conflict.

The URC (later called URHC for United Refugee and Host Churches) began by saying that the conflict between churches was undermining their witness and that God expected better of them. They brought a group together to discuss the problem and to agree on a theology of cooperation, trust, and compassion that would be the basis for their shared ministry. Their core theology was that God expected them to sacrifice for others in need, care for the most vulnerable among them, and demonstrate servant leadership.

The URHC implemented their theology by first forming a central committee composed of elected pastors. This committee would oversee donations to the URHC and be responsible for sharing the donations equitably. This not only reduced disagreements about managing donations but also increased donations by providing a single point of contact for outside agencies. Further, the committee demonstrated a commitment to trust and servant leadership by

---

1. This story is based on a study by D. Boan, B. Andrews, K. Sanders, D. Martinson, E. Loewer, J. Aten, 2018.

operating openly and deferring its interests until those of other group members were satisfied.

Building on this foundation, the URHC went on to implement several key strategies to build their community:

Reducing Barriers

One of the first tasks of the URHC was to reduce barriers between people and their groups (tribes, denominations, etc.). They did this by promoting communication and sharing between groups. Later, this effort extended outside of their camp to the surrounding Turkana host community LFCs (hence the name change to URHC), leading to several Turkana community LFCs joining the URHC.

Serve the Vulnerable

Even in a place where all people are vulnerable, the URHC recognized that there were several extremely vulnerable groups: divorcees, children, the disabled, and widows. Giving for the sake of the vulnerable was a basic expression of the faith of the URHC members and a demonstration of the role of the LFC in the community. Even with reduced food supplies, members tithed from their food to care for others. This was widely seen as a convincing sign of the faith and values of the group and one of the key activities that established them as a major influence in the community.

Conflict Resolution

Once the URHC established itself as a trusted entity in the camp, they moved on to address conflict and promote peace. They began teaching conflict resolution skills, and appointed community liaisons who would be close to the community and recognize signs of developing conflict. These liaisons would then act as trusted arbitrators and intervene in local conflicts, whether between LFCs, within LFCs, or within families.

Communication

Communication is another core activity of the URHC and an important aspect of connecting with the community. Conflict typically starts with rumor and distorted communication, all the more so in an environment where people see pervasive injustice. The URHC positioned itself as a source of reliable and trusted information, and it regularly confronted distorted stories and rumors. In this way, this LFC group established itself as a source of truth.

Women and Children

Two groups received special attention from the URHC as the most vulnerable among them: women and children. For children, the URHC regularly taught the proper care of children, confronted abuse, and launched special programs to provide care and support for children. Special attention was given to children separated from their parents by conflict. These children received special supervision and support. Further, regular youth camps operated during the year so that children would have a place to build relationships with the church members who wished to support them.

Women received attention as a group that, culturally, was often maltreated. The URHC's theology regarding women began with the belief that, in God, there was no male or female, and thus, both sexes should receive equal treatment. Equality was a major culture change task that is still ongoing. In a culture that puts women at a disadvantage, the URHC did not merely allow women to assume important roles and participate in the life of the LFC but actively reached out to women to help them to participate. The URHC recruited women to receive formal education and participate in leadership. In addition to biblical and theological education, women were taught business skills.

In sum, this association of churches in a refugee camp demonstrates how translating basic beliefs into action can have a profound impact on a community. In this case, although not entirely due to the URHC, Kakuma is one of the most peaceful refugee camps in the world. The conflict between churches has all but ended, and other conflicts have diminished significantly.

The URHC is even recognized by the UN as a major contributor to the quality of life in the camp and surrounding community.

Authors' Comments

The case story about the URHC illustrates the four key practices (seeking justice, building social capital, promoting engagement, creating restoration) and describes the impact these had in a challenging community setting. It is noteworthy that the URHC created engagement and participation by first confronting corruption and injustice. They insisted on transparency and required leaders to defer receiving resources until all others were satisfied with the distribution. The community realized that corruption was the root of injustice and that they could not have justice and build trust without eliminating corruption.

The URHC also built social capital through the creation of the network, as well as through the school they established and the system of community elders they introduced. The social systems they constructed were the architecture through which they then implemented their mission.

Finally, the story also illustrates restoration. This is an interesting and unexpected element in a setting where resources are extremely scarce. The theology of the group was that Scripture teaches us to share what we have – regardless of how much that is – and to share without respect to boundaries (as in Christ's teaching about who is our neighbor). Thus, they implemented resource sharing across the larger community without respect to faith, tribal affiliation or geography.

An Example from Egypt: The Alexandria Youth Committee (AYC)[2]
Background

The following case story is based on interviews conducted with Mr Maged Milad, Development Director for the Alexandria Youth Committee (AYC), in August and September 2017. The purpose of this case story is to describe strategies, insights, and lessons that might be helpful to others working in the field of faith-based community development. Key terms and background information were supplemented from documents provided to the interviewers. Sections in quotes are from the interview with Milad.

Interview/History

The Alexandria Youth Committee (AYC) was founded in 1987 to serve young adults in universities among evangelical LFCs in Alexandria.[3] The youth were seen as needing "mentors, discipleship, and training in how to be effective in their community." LFCs lacked such programming, having adopted a way of preaching which promoted knowledge but not practices so that "churches became filled by audiences but not participants." Milad described the mindset of the church as seeing Christ providing forgiveness and nothing more. Often,

---

2. Maged Milad, interview by David Boan and Weston Kinsinger, Wheaton, Illinois, March 23, 2018.

3. From the AYC Website http://the-ayc.com/.

members of the church were inactive in their neighboring communities. They did not believe that their Christian faith necessitated any active transformation in their relationship with the secular community. This mindset led churches to be uninvolved in their communities and to separate themselves from their neighbors.

The Community Development sector of the AYC was initiated in January 2011. At that time, there was a belief that the broken relationship and barriers between the church and the neighboring Muslim communities would eventually lead to greater hostility and even violent attacks against churches. The members of the AYC believed that the current approach to discipleship and evangelism for youth was insufficient to mend the broken relationship and reduce the barriers between the church and the Muslim and secular communities.

"We started the Community Development sector as a way to build up the relationship between the church and the community." The AYC attempted several programs to improve the living conditions of the communities. First, they initiated a garment manufacturing program, teaching participants about making and selling garments, then helping them start their own businesses. Next, the AYC initiated providing sustainable development with hydroponics systems to villages outside the city of Alexandria. Lastly, they started a microfinance model to help finance "not what we [AYC] see is good for them, but what they see is good for them."

None of the AYC initiatives were sustained. Participants depended upon the consultants of the AYC to market their products. "Though they made many products, they still were unable to penetrate the market by themselves. They needed our consultant each time." In addition, microfinancing was also very difficult in the city and slum communities because they were vulnerable to foreign currency fluctuations. Any change in the dollar affected the local economy. The small businesses were unprepared to maintain themselves in volatile markets and depended upon the AYC for continued support. Though the AYC provided financial support for community-initiated projects and coaching to participant groups, "the challenges were bigger than the support we provided." The programs were not self-sustaining.

While the AYC programs helped many people, their success depended upon the continued support of the AYC. The method they used reinforced the impoverished identity and dependency of the participants. It communicated that "you [the participants] are powerless and you are poor. We [AYC] have the resources, we have all things, we know all things, and we have the rights. So you have to obey us. You have to listen to your teachers and do what we say."

The book *When Helping Hurts* was formative for AYC leaders at a time when they were struggling to sustain their efforts. "At this time, I was making a lot of medical outreaches and the blood donations, trying to improve the people and to improve their lives, to provide donation, and to provide healthcare for people. A lot of good things for the people, not just for missions." After reading *When Helping Hurts,* however, they realized that "we should not map the need in the community, but we should map the assets and the resources in the community."

What was needed was collective action. Collective action is the initiative of communities to identify their shared needs and goals so that they can then organize themselves to fulfill those needs and accomplish those goals. According to Maged:

> At this stage, we discovered that we do not have to teach people a lot to make them teach themselves in collective action, collective thinking. However, we have to take collective action because as individuals, it is easy to think, but as a group [it] is harder to think. Thinking and acting as a group helps to empower people to make something sustainable.

The AYC staff had no experience in collective action so, using Google, they found the COUDY Institute. The COUDY Institute offers a six-month course on collective thinking and action in development, offering sixteen specified programs dedicated to educating "leaders in development from around the world."[4] The general focus of the courses was on the application of participatory approaches to "equip citizen leaders to address contemporary global challenges and opportunities."[5] The program in which Milad enrolled was "Asset-Based and Citizen-Led Development." More specific topics covered in this program included: implementing citizen-led and asset-based principles in an organization; innovative forms of "member-based organizations as vehicles for sustainable community-led activity"; and developing citizen-led initiatives through multi-stakeholder platforms and by linking producers to markets.[6]

As part of these courses, Milad developed his church-based model of development. "The model is related to transforming the identity of the people in the church to be able to transform the community, and to engage

---

4. From the COUDY institute website http://www.coady.stfx.ca/education/programs/.

5. http://www.coady.stfx.ca/education/programs/.

6. http://www.coady.stfx.ca/tinroom/assets/file/ABCD_2018.pdf.

the community in collective thinking and collective action without putting our agendas on them." Milad returned to Alexandria and the AYC with ideas for new methods that encourage participants to be actors and not just audiences.

In order for a group or program to be sustainable, they must be able to think collectively to resolve their problems. The focus of the AYC was now to generate a new mindset, emphasizing active Christian attitudes, values, and behaviors. They engaged youth and those not in leadership positions in the church in discipleship groups to teach this mindset through interactive and experiential learning. Discipleship groups engaged one another in discussions through interactive learning to identify what they thought as a community and not just as individuals. The objective of the AYC was to have the discipleship groups practice collective thinking by responding as a group to discipleship materials and questions of faith. This collective focus was intended to promote self-sustaining practices within the groups.

Experiential learning is a necessity

> because if the people in the discipleship groups listen to our teaching and pray, at the time of community development, they will do nothing. They will continue listening. However, if we put the DNA of the engagement of the participatory approach and the collective thinking and the collective action at day one of the discipleship groups, then they will be learning by doing. So, we engage the LFCs to be able to generate knowledge to assert biblical values.

The AYC now provides opportunities for discipleship groups to serve their communities. It organizes medical outreach and blood drives, as well as food, clothing, and medical supply distribution. It encourages members of the discipleship group to form the habit of service and to generate positive experiences from active participation in the church and the community. Groups that participate in these programs develop trust and a credible reputation with the community at large. Groups are also able to gather community stakeholders from different levels and include them in the process of collective thinking and the participatory approach to development. The end products of this process are bottom-up projects of sustainable community development to meet the community needs.

As trust within local communities grew, the programs became more sustainable and began to spread. The AYC then came to the attention of other faith groups, particularly the Muslim community. Muslim community members noticed the benefits to the community and approached the AYC to discuss the possibility of collaborating with them. Currently, the AYC is working across faith groups in serving the community as well as in teaching their church- and faith-based collective model to other groups.

Challenges

One challenge that arises is when the AYC asks the churches for feedback. Churches will ask the AYC to come back to train the needy through the same discipleship groups they provided to the churches. The AYC responds to these requests by saying, "please do not ask us again to teach any needy people." They must learn to teach themselves if the AYC is to avoid making the same mistake of having communities be continually dependent on the AYC for teaching.

Another challenge is meeting the expectations of the people. One of the goals of the AYC is to build a relationship with the church and the community at large by strengthening the trust and credibility of the church. It is critical that the AYC builds up the credibility of the church, but this also means that the community will have expectations of the church.

> We build up the trust in the community, and the community trusts that the church will do much work. So, the risk of collective action is that we raise the expectations of the people. Then and you have to spend all your time to try and manage their expectations, not to meet their need but also meet their expectation. We have a workforce dedicated to meeting the expectations and dreams of the people, but much time and resources are spent to meet the community's expectations, not necessarily their needs. The workforce is insufficient to coordinate all the different projects. So the problem is not in the community; the problem is the organization and the church. We do not have enough people who are capable and professional to work with the community.

The final challenge relates to how well participating churches follow the AYC model. The AYC model has four stages, and each stage has written materials. While the LFCs do much great work, they tend not to include all the parts of the model. This is a challenge. So the AYC evaluates and provides feedback for the programs they organize to improve the church's community involvement. "The participants' expectation is that they will bring the church from nothing to put on a professional evangelism event aimed at engaging people in the journey of Christ. We know that it is hard for the church; they are just beginning. We accept this situation. Sometimes the church is aligned with our approach, but we accept them." Feedback is provided with the understanding that the church is not a professional organization. The feedback aims to communicate to the churches what the AYC expects, with a view to help them develop their ability to serve their communities.

An Example from Lebanon: Good Practices in Faith-Sensitive Innovation to Build Integrated Communities[7]
Introduction

This case study is part of a collaborative project carried out by the Joint Learning Initiative and the United Nations High Commissioner for Refugees (UNHCR), which aims to generate locally grounded evidence and identify examples of good practices of local faith community-led responses to refugees across six countries: Honduras, Mexico, Uganda, Germany, Bangladesh, and Lebanon. Thirty-five interviews and one focus group among a total of 46 participants were conducted for this case study.[8]

Based in Mansourieh El Maten, MERATH (Middle East Revive & Thrive) is the relief and community development arm of the Lebanese Society for Educational and Social Development (LSESD). MERATH partners with local churches and Faith-Based Organizations (FBOs) in Lebanon, Syria, and Iraq to support humanitarian and development interventions across basic needs, education and child protection, livelihoods and local partner capacity building. MERATH does not currently partner with local Muslim faith communities or FBOs, but services are provided to all regardless of ethnicity or religion. This case study details some of the ways in which MERATH and its partners demonstrate good practices in refugee response.

---

7. Contributed by Middle East Revive and Thrive (MERATH, https://merathlebanon.org/), the relief and development arm of the Lebanese Society for Educational and Social Development (LSESD, http://www.lsesd.org/); also published on UNHCR's Comprehensive Refugee Response Framework (CRRF, http://www.globalcrrf.org/crrf_good_practices/) Global Digital Portalin collaboration with the Joint Learning Initiative on Faith & Local Communities (JLIFLC, https://jliflc.com/).

8. PROJECT LEADS: Prof. Elena Fiddian-Qasmiyeh, University College London, and Dr. Olivia Wilkinson, Joint Learning Initiative on Faith and Local Communities (JLI), with significant research contribution from Leonie Harsch, and analysis and writing from Molly Middlehurst and Heather Wurtz.

Support for Host Communities

Due to the complicated history of Syrian political and military intervention in Lebanon, many hosts and local faith leaders (LFLs) reported significant resistance and reluctance to supporting Syrian refugees in Lebanon. Many hosts expressed their frustration at the increasing numbers of Syrian refugees in Lebanon and felt that they were a strain on limited resources. Lack of employment opportunities and the influx of cheap Syrian and refugee labor undercutting Lebanese living wages were also often cited as a major concern for hosts and a tension between the communities. Many hosts, LFLs and some refugees expressed the belief that direct service provision and material support to host communities in need would be key to disrupting tensions that arose with the influx of Syrian refugees.

In order to navigate strained relations, some LFLs have adopted new strategies that also include support for host communities. One church, for example, was providing basic food items in baskets to Syrian refugees; however, they found that the high demand and difficulty in distribution caused further friction with the local community. So, they began going directly to Lebanese neighbors to offer some of the same support they had been providing to refugees.

> We also heard many people [from the local community] say "why are you only helping them, we are also in need." So we helped all those who are in need and went to all of the neighbors and gave them a food basket. This is how we solved this problem. Some of the neighbors said that they are not in need, but most of them took the food basket and were very happy. When doctors are visiting us, we send messages to all the neighbors and say that they can come for medical assistance, and they come. So instead of being against us, they thank us for what we do. They now know that we care for everyone; that we try to help everyone and that we love everyone.

As prominent local actors, religious leaders and their churches are closer to these criticisms than more external humanitarian organizations. Although they must constantly navigate these tensions to retain their trusted positions in communities, they may also be particularly well-positioned to help bridge divides across social difference through innovative, peacebuilding practices that respond to local challenges and needs.

Spiritual Support and Religious Motivations

LFLs and FBO employees also play a critical role in enhancing refugee self-reliance through psychosocial and spiritual intervention. Both refugees and Lebanese hosts mentioned the importance of home visits where LFLs or NGOs were able to see the circumstances and needs of refugees first hand and provide various forms of psychosocial support, from guidance on ways to adapt and integrate into a new society to prayers and spiritual counsel. One male refugee described feeling cared for and less alone because of in-home visits: "They come, pray for us, invite us, say that they hope with us that we can return to our country. This is also a form of support. They care for us and visit us and share our worries. It makes us feel a bit more comfortable that there are people who follow up on us and greet us." Another male refugee who has been in Lebanon for six years described members of a church visiting his home and engaging him in interfaith conversations: "When the people from the church visit, they give us lessons on cleanliness and religion, and they pray. We have a conversation about religion, between them as Christians and us as Sunnites."

Many hosts and LFLs cited religious teachings and values as motivation to support refugees, despite initial resistance and across religious differences. Indeed, many LFLs and hosts felt their religious affiliation and teachings compelled them not only to provide material support to refugees but also to act out of compassion, forgiveness, and "love." According to one male faith leader:

> Faith plays an important role in my relationship with refugees because it is the major motivation for offering assistance to them. If there were not our belief in Christ, we would not work with refugees. We respect the holy gospel, and it is the basis of our faith and our life. The gospel teaches us to help the hungry, the ill, the persecuted, and those who are displaced from their homes. We assist refugees because the gospel teaches us to do so. We do this work with love and not as a duty. In addition to the [material] assistance, we offer love to refugees.

The relationships between hosts and refugees include discussions of religion and emotions, which are potentially highly sensitive topics. International and external organizations consider that it is good practice to exercise impartiality and neutrality, often resulting in the avoidance of religion to maintain distance from perceived affiliation among refugees with partial parties.[9] However, as the Lebanon case demonstrates, an approach in which LFLs can express their religious beliefs while also respecting the beliefs of others can help create a supportive environment for refugees of diverse religious backgrounds. Local faith actors may affirm their impartiality in assistance by helping all and not discriminating in their services, while also engaging in prayer, discussing religious similarities and differences, and speaking about emotional and spiritual topics with displaced people.

One female respondent who traveled from Syria to Lebanon as a refugee sixteen years ago and told the interviewer she still identifies as a refugee rather than a member of the local/host community, reported feeling welcome by Christian faith leaders even though she is Sunni:

> The people who serve in the church have hearts which are maybe like the heart of Jesus Christ. They resemble Jesus because they do not want to see anyone being sad, tired, or in need. I did not see anyone like them; they are wonderful. A friend of my husband informed us about the church, and I came there. They received me and welcomed me. They are very respectful. I am Sunni, but I liked them.

Another female refugee from Syria echoed this sentiment: "I am Muslim, but when I attend prayers, it comforts me spiritually and emotionally. [It comforts me] when they give me patience in daily life with the community of the country in which I am living." This acknowledges the agency of refugees and the local faith actors in host communities to engage in complex and nuanced relationships in which faith plays a supportive role.

Local faith actors are often on the front lines of promoting theinclusion and resilience of refugee populations. Acknowledging that some local faith actors can also reinforce exclusionary practices, the research presented in this case study has instead pointed towards good practice examples in which local faith actors have led their wider communities to challenge discrimination against displaced people and promote their social integration. Local faith actors can stand against populist currents to call for the population around them to welcome the stranger; this can be through teaching from scriptural bases but

---

9. Alastair Ager and Joey Ager, *Faith, Secularism, and Humanitarian Engagement: Finding the Place of Religion in the Support of Displaced Communities* (New York: Palgrave Macmillan, 2015); Olivia Wilkinson, "'Faith Can Come In, but Not Religion': Secularity and Its Effects on the Disaster Response to Typhoon Haiyan," *Disasters* 42, no. 3 (October 24, 2017): 459–474, https://doi.org/10.1111/disa.12258.

also by working from the social and spiritual capital of faith communities to act for inclusion rather than marginalization.

Key Reflections from the Comprehensive Refugee Response Framework good practices database

- Material assistance of residents, such as food distribution, along with refugee aid, provides support for host communities while promoting social cohesion by easing tensions between host and refugee groups.
- Interventions of faith-based organizations, such as home visits and interfaith dialogue, enhance refugee self-reliance and inclusivity.
- Despite the attempts of many organizations to avoid religious activities in order to maintain impartiality, this case demonstrates the role of spirituality in creating a supportive environment and dignified reception conditions for refugees, as well as promoting resilience and respect for diversity throughout the local community.

An Example from Cameroon: Ending Child Marriage[10]
Background

On 3 March 2017, Bishop Dibo Elango was interviewed about his work related to engaging congregations and communities in ending violence against children. This and other stories are part of a campaign to end violence against children and serve to provide faith leaders seeking to join the campaign with a vision of what is possible.

Interview

The Rt Rev Dibo Elango is the Bishop of Cameroon, an Anglican diocese that oversees the entire nation of Cameroon. Bishop Dibo became a deacon in the Anglican church in 1999 and, in 2000, was ordained as a priest. In 2008, he was appointed Bishop of Cameroon and was in this role at the time of this interview (2017). Though he now holds the position of bishop, he still sees himself in the role of a deacon – a servant to the congregation. In his own words, "we remain deacons even when we are bishops, and we will not forget that."

Bishop Dibo shared information about Cameroon and the history of the LFC in Cameroon. "The story of Cameroon is different because we have

---

10. From unpublished research conducted by David Boan and Weston Kinsinger, March 2017.

never had missionaries here from Europe." Instead of missionaries, members of the Anglican church from Nigeria, Togo, Liberia, and Ghana brought the Anglican church and the Anglican tradition to Cameroon. "They were God's people who would love us and our farms," says Bishop Dibo, adding that "[the Cameroonians] wanted to worship with the Anglicans." He continues, "they started building churches. When they called for oversight from the Archbishop of Canterbury they were placed under the Anglican Province of West Africa."

Bishop Dibo ascribes the unique history of the church in Cameroon to the variety of denominational traditions present in the Anglican church of Cameroon today. There are many Anglicans, and also evangelicals, charismatics, and pentecostals. "So, it is a blend of all. We make sure that we live within that blend, accommodating to one another's way and respecting one another's way of worshiping God. We try and make sure that our services are inclusive."

Bishop Dibo began to involve the diocese of Cameroon in the protection of children in 2012, after he and his wife, Estel, attended a training program sponsored by the Mothers' Union. Bishop Dibo and Estel implemented the skills and techniques they learned through this program in the programs already in place in the diocese.

Bishop Dibo gave two reasons for engaging the church in the protection of children. First and foremost, he said, it was the church's duty to do so; second, he saw the great needs of children. Bishop Dibo saw "challenges that drove the movement." There were many injustices in Cameroon about which the church did not speak up, including juvenile delinquency and sexual assault of children.

Bishop Dibo explained how he viewed the mission of the church in relation to child protection. The government does provide materials and policies on the proper care and protection of children. The policies are "okay," but they were not adequately implemented by the government and thus failed to address the issue of child-raising and child protection. The church differs from the government in that "we saw ourselves . . . as able to add our voice, to add our action, to add whatever we can add to ensure this vision [of protecting children and respecting childhood]." The church is like a moralist, training the internal judgment of people and how to raise their children. The church also provides informal education not under the control of the government. This enables the church to add to the government materials and provide alternative means for implementing policies.

One example of the church's efforts for child protection is the annual five-day theater festival. The festival is an opportunity to raise awareness of the prevalence of child maltreatment and inform the public of available preventative measures. The festival includes girls marching with T-shirts reading "Save Our Girls." They carry placards describing "vices" or behaviors that endanger children, as well as ways to keep children, especially girls, safe. This festival started as an annual program but grew to the point where it was possible to have multiple marches in different cities around Cameroon.

Another part of this vision is the Alpha Force. Alpha Forces seek to empower individuals by encouraging self-value and promoting public health and healthy relationships. There are groups for youth, for women, and for married couples. There is a huge need for this program in Cameroon, especially for married couples, and churches and civil society frequently request that the program be run.

Alpha for marriage is one of the more popular programs, led by Estel Elango, the wife of Bishop Dibo Elango. Mrs Elango shared that couples learn how to "conduct [themselves] in marriages to take care of their children and also to make sure that they are a part of this greater mission" (i.e. learn how they can support the larger national effort to protect children). In these groups, young married couples are counseled in healthy monogamous marriages and guided to set marriage goals, resolve conflict, and practice family planning. The issue of polygamous marriages is also addressed. The goal of these programs is creating healthy families that are dedicated to raising children to their full capacity.

The church operates the Girls Friendly Society, a youth organization operating in churches throughout Cameroon and other nations. The girls who are now a part of these groups were the same girls who participated in the children's first marches years ago. The groups provide support for girls through young adulthood. Once a year, they host a retreat or camp for teenage girls. For three to five days, the girls attend sessions on sexual health, marriage, and motherhood, as well as abortion, rape, incest, and unplanned pregnancies. They are made aware of resources dealing with prevention and support. Speakers, who have been through some of these issues, are brought together and present their testimonies to educate and encourage the girls. They emphasize that the girls should not keep silent but speak out if they face such issues. One of the key slogans used is: "Do not keep silent! Speak out!" These testimonies are recorded on CDs so that the girls can listen to them once they are back at home or school. Through these retreats, the girls are introduced to resources that will help them as they go on into adulthood.

Members and teachers within the church congregation run these programs and Bishop Dibo and Mrs Elango devote a great deal of time to training them. Teachers are trained in "didactics" – teaching with the intent of moral instruction.

Bishop Dibo and Mrs Elango face several challenges. One is learning to work with the limited materials available. They discovered that when they used the available materials for training, participants would provide further examples and add to the materials.

When asked what advice he would give to groups seeking to begin a program like his, Bishop Dibo responded that the individuals must have a structure that organizes and guides individual efforts. It is important to have a clear structure for the program that provides support for different actions, such as collaborating with others. It is also important to recognize that there is one mission, and the church is just one of the organizations with that mission. Though the church is trusted by the people, and could act alone, it is still important to work with other organizations. And working well with other organizations requires a clear structure that the other organizations can interact with.

Working in education can also be challenging due to the need to collaborate with the government. The government of Cameroon has a designated education program and provides some materials for it. Bishop Dibo and the Mothers' Union use the government materials and work with the government, but they also add many ministries such as family education, secondary and high school education, and moral education. Since they work in education, the government provides a small amount of financial support, but it is still very difficult to finance the programs. "We do not gain; we just serve and hope God will maintain."

When asked how change has been brought about within the church, Bishop Dibo shared how he himself is an example of how the work has brought about change. Before his bishopric, Bishop Dibo was a classroom teacher. In his work as a teacher, Bishop Dibo sought excellence in his teaching and in the performance of his students. This taught his students to value both the learning and teaching dimensions of education. Bishop Dibo shares how this value continues to this day through many of his students, now grown, who have joined him in the church's mission. Some who join in the church's mission are not Anglicans. Bishop Dibo emphasized that the mission for protecting children "has nothing to do with the denomination. It has everything to do with what God wants!"

Bishop Dibo notes that another challenge is the divisions between the denominations. In responding to these challenges, he affirms the importance of centering the teaching on Christ and the mission. Having Christ-centered and mission-oriented teaching can change both the speaker and the audience. It has a "two-way agency," as we must learn from one another and we all must change as we go towards what God has asked of us, as we go towards making the world a better and safer place. Only what has come from God and is centered in his truth will last till the end. As we continue to follow God in this way, all that is not from God and is not true will fall away. "So let the mistakes pass because the words they are carrying are the words of God. God will bid them be heard some way. So, as they are passing through challenges, they should know about that because in the future, these challenges will go away, and we will see how our God will prevail."

Bishop Dibo advises being mindful of two things. First, he says, we must remain grounded and be mindful of what is before us, of the circumstances of the people (both children and adults). Parental discord, single parents, orphans, and street children are some of the situations and individuals Bishop Dibo and the Mothers' Union seek to minister to. Second, develop every child's skills. There are no hopeless children or hopeless situations. "If they discover that skill and if justice is done, we will have less violence and vice in society. Everybody would be a voice for one another and be a helper when they see any situation which is not normal." Asked about leadership, Bishop Dibo describes how he and Mrs Elango are very dependent upon the people in the church for leadership. "We are Christ's family," he explains, "and whether they are older than me or younger than Mrs Elango, we need them because we need different people in the church every day."

Lessons and Insights

From the interview, we made several observations that are relevant to the role of the church in the community. First, the members of the participating churches formed the core of the program. They became the teachers, organizers, and resource developers. This last group – those developing resources – struck us as particularly creative. The average person has many stories that can make a curriculum more powerful by making it more personal and contextually relevant.

Bishop Dibo affirmed the central role played by the church in providing structure for the program. This role is an important element when considering church-based community programs. Services require structure. Quite often, an NGO provides that structure even though the church or church networks are quite capable of providing it. A church-based structure differs from an NGO structure in important ways. As Bishop Dibo noted, their programming integrated with other church services, such as Sunday school and the church camp. It also added an element of moral teaching, integrated stories from members, and helped to contextualize the content.

The interfaith aspect of this program also offers an important lesson. Bishop Dibo promoted interfaith cooperation by emphasizing the shared elements of faith and theology, and he avoided conflicts by stressing that God was in control and would work with, and through, their various efforts.

We observe how the children were helped to become advocates for themselves through the marches and placards. Engaging children in this way not only provides a way to empower them but is also likely to be a powerful demonstration to all members of the community that organizing and advocating for themselves is within their reach.

Finally, this program worked in cooperation with the national government. It advanced the government policy by recognizing that the government policy was failing and that this created an opportunity for the church to become involved and demonstrate its capacity to change society.

In sum, we found this to be an excellent demonstration of the power of a church network to bring about social change through programs that were implemented in a well-organized, creative, and thoughtful way.

Authors' Comment

The story of confronting child marriage in Cameroon illustrates important elements of social capital, seeking justice, and engagement. First, the problem was framed as a justice issue. Early marriages deprive children of their childhood, exploit them, and are abusive. The social capital of the church (churches with Sunday school classes, Bible studies, and youth programs) became a means of engaging people in the issue. Materials were developed and programs implemented through this structure. As support for the program grew, additional social capital developed, including camps for youth and a youth march – which are forms of social capital. It is noteworthy that government support was also engaged to support this by aligning the campaign with existing (and largely unenforced) laws against early marriage.

6

Conclusions

Resilience models offer useful insights into the constructive interactions between the faith community, individuals, and the community at large. They show us how the lives of all community members are interconnected, that barriers between groups have consequences for the entire community, and that the response to those in crisis becomes part of the story about the community in its entirety. Thus, resilience is not a church program or some capacity that needs development. It is also not a fad, jargon, or challenge to the LFC to be something other than what it is. It is a way to understand the important dynamics that are ongoing aspects of the relationship between the faith community, individuals, and the community at large.

The connection between the LFC and the resilience of individuals and communities is not only clear and vital; we have described it as a role that LFCs are in a unique position to fulfill. LFCs are not organizations that work in the community; they *are* the community, or at least a part of it. This distinction fundamentally determines the efficacy of resilience-building activities by LFCs in ways that are different from any other organization. First, LFCs have a powerful role in shaping the meaning that community members attach to events. They do this in multiple ways: through informal worship as a leader speaks from the pulpit, in the education of members, and in dialogues that take place among members in many settings, both formal and informal. Second, by being part of the community, LFCs shape the dialogue and meaning developed in the community at large. This is especially true when LFCs are actively engaged in the life of the community, respond to the needs of community members, and respond to critical events in a meaningful and timely way.

Understanding resilience can help leaders see that the dynamic processes that underlie resilience are dynamics that have the potential to be either constructive or destructive. For LFCs, this is a way to review the consequences of certain actions and understand their larger impacts.

Where Do We Go from Here?

There are signs that the church is rediscovering justice, along with disturbing signs that it still has a long way to go. The news about the cover-up of child abuse in the church – both Catholic and Protestant churches – demonstrates that justice is secondary to public appearances. The fact that people who abuse children are among the leaders of the church is not the main concern, for abusers exist in every segment of society and likely always will. The greater concern is that an institution dedicated to justice would know that abuse is occurring and fail to confront the perpetrators and demand justice for victims – some considered this a symptom of a long-standing failure to seek justice. For example, in *Reconstructing the Gospel: Finding Freedom from Slaveholder Religion*, Wilson-Hartgrove makes the case that the roots of injustice lie in the church's relationship with slavery in the USA.[1] In the 1800s, churches discounted the injustice of slavery so that they could support slavery. That corruption of the biblical call to seek justice continued through the Jim Crow era, through the battle for civil rights, and, to this day, in the cover-up of abuse and even in the denial of support for immigrants. We see brighter signs of hope in the Southern Baptist Convention's public report on their history of abuse cover-up, the Pope's confronting abuse in the Catholic church, and the networks of churches working on humanitarian issues. We hope that this book will contribute to this ongoing discussion and help church leaders and para-church groups reclaim the church's identity as a window into God's just community.

---

1. Wilson-Hartgrove, *Reconstructing the Gospel.*

Appendix A

Creation Care and the Gospel: Jamaica Call to Action[1]

1. A new commitment to a simple lifestyle. Recognizing that much of our crisis is due to billions of lives lived carelessly, we reaffirm the Lausanne commitment to simple lifestyle (Lausanne Occasional Paper 20), and call on the global evangelical community to take steps, personally and collectively, to live within the proper boundaries of God's good gift in creation, to engage further in its restoration and conservation, and to equitably share its bounty with each other.

2. New and robust theological work. In particular, we need guidance in four areas:

- An integrated theology of creation care that can engage seminaries, Bible colleges, and others to equip pastors to disciple their congregations.
- A theology that examines humanity's identity as both embedded in creation and yet possessing a special role toward creation.
- A theology that challenges current prevailing economic ideologies in relation to our biblical stewardship of creation.
- A theology of hope in Christ and his Second Coming that properly informs and inspires creation care.

3. Leadership from the church in the Global South. As the Global South represents those most affected in the current ecological crisis, it possesses a particular need to speak up, engage issues of creation care, and act upon them. We the members of the Consultation further request that the church of the Global South exercise leadership among us, helping to set the agenda for the advance of the gospel and the care of creation.

---

1. This appendix taken from https://www.lausanne.org/content/statement/creation-care-call-to-action.

4. Mobilization of the whole church and engagement of all of society. Mobilization must occur at the congregational level and include those who are often overlooked, utilizing the gifts of women, children, youth, and indigenous people as well as professionals and other resource people who possess experience and expertise. Engagement must be equally widespread, including formal, urgent, and creative conversations with responsible leaders in government, business, civil society, and academia.

5. Environmental missions among unreached people groups. We participate in Lausanne's historic call to world evangelization, and believe that environmental issues represent one of the greatest opportunities to demonstrate the love of Christ and plant churches among unreached and unengaged people groups in our generation. We encourage the church to promote "environmental missions" as a new category within mission work (akin in function to medical missions).

6. Radical action to confront climate change. Affirming the Cape Town Commitment's declaration of the "serious and urgent challenge of climate change" which will "disproportionately affect those in poorer countries" . . ., we call for action in radically reducing greenhouse gas emissions and building resilient communities. We understand these actions to be an application of the command to deny ourselves, take up the cross. and follow Christ.

7. Sustainable principles in food production. In gratitude to God who provides sustenance, and flowing from our conviction to become excellent stewards of creation, we urge the application of environmentally and generationally sustainable principles in agriculture (field crops and livestock, fisheries and all other forms of food production), with particular attention to the use of methodologies such as conservation agriculture.

8. An economy that works in harmony with God's creation. We call for an approach to economic well-being and development, energy production, natural resource management (including mining and forestry), water management and use, transportation, health care, rural and urban design and living, and personal and corporate consumption patterns that maintain the ecological integrity of creation.

9. Local expressions of creation care, which preserve and enhance biodiversity. We commend such projects, along with any action that might be characterized as the "small step" or the "symbolic act," to the worldwide church as ways to powerfully witness to Christ's lordship over all creation.

10. Prophetic advocacy and healing reconciliation. We call for individual Christians and the church as a whole to prophetically "speak the truth to power" through advocacy and legal action so that public policies and private practice may change to better promote the care of creation and better support devastated communities and habitats. Additionally, we call the church to "speak the peace of Christ" into communities torn apart by environmental disputes, mobilizing those who are skilled at conflict resolution, and maintaining our own convictions with humility.

Appendix B

Conservation of Resource Theory – List of Resources[1]

There are various approaches to defining resources, and it is important to recognize that resources are also culturally dependent. Thus, the following list is provided as an illustration and is not meant to be the definitive list for all settings.

1. Personal transportation (car, truck, etc.)
2. Feeling that I am successful
3. Time for adequate sleep
4. Good marriage
5. Adequate clothing
6. Feeling valuable to others
7. Family stability
8. Free time
9. More clothing than I need
10. Sense of pride in myself
11. Intimacy with one or more family members
12. Time for work
13. Feeling that I am accomplishing my goals
14. Good relationship with my children
15. Time with loved ones
16. Necessary tools for work
17. Hope
18. Children's health
19. Stamina/endurance

---

1. Taken from J. D. Snyder, D. Boan, J. D. Aten, E. B. Davis, L. Van Grinsven, T. Liu, and E. L. Worthington Jr. "Resource Loss and Stress Outcomes in a Setting of Chronic Conflict: The Conservation of Resources Theory in the Eastern Congo." *Journal of Traumatic Stress* (2019). https://doi.org/10.1002/jts.22448.

20. Necessary home appliances
21. Feeling that my future success depends on me
22. Positively challenging routine
23. Personal health
24. Housing that suits my needs
25. Sense of optimism
26. Status/seniority at work
27. Adequate food
28. Larger home than I need
29. Sense of humor
30. Stable employment
31. Intimacy with spouse or partner
32. Adequate home furnishings
33. Feeling that I have control over my life
34. Role as a leader
35. Ability to communicate well
36. Ability to provide my children's essentials
37. Feeling that my life is peaceful
38. Acknowledgement of my accomplishments
39. Ability to organize tasks
40. Extras for children
41. Sense of commitment
42. Intimacy with at least one friend
43. Money for extras
44. Self-discipline
45. Understanding from my employer/boss
46. Savings or emergency money
47. Motivation to get things done
48. Spouse/partner's health
49. Support from coworkers
50. Adequate income
51. Feeling that I know who I am
52. Advancement in education or job training
53. Adequate financial credit
54. Feeling independent
55. Companionship
56. Financial assets (stocks, property, etc.)
57. Knowing where I am going with my life
58. Affection from others

59. Financial stability
60. Feeling that my life has meaning/purpose
61. Positive feelings about myself
62. People I can learn from
63. Money for transportation
64. Help with tasks at work
65. Medical insurance
66. Involvement with church, synagogue, etc.
67. Retirement security (financial)
68. Help with tasks at home
69. Loyalty of friends
70. Money for advancement or self-improvement (education, starting a business, etc.)
71. Help with child care
72. Involvement in organizations with others who have similar interests
73. Financial help if needed
74. Health of family/close friends

Appendix C

Disaster Ministry and Risk Reduction Resources

Aten, J. and D. Boan. *Handbook of Disaster Ministry*. InterVarsity Press: Wheaton, 2006.

Food for the Hungry. *Church Leaders Training Manual*. 2014.

Food for the Hungry. *Community Leaders Training Manual*. 2014.

Tearfund LEARN Resources available at: https://learn.tearfund.org/en.

Sample: Tearfund (2011) *Disasters and the Local Church: Guidelines for Church Leaders in Disaster-Prone Areas.*

World Relief. *A Church Leader's Tool Kit on the Syrian Refugee Crisis*. Available at https://worldrelief.org/church-leaders-toolkit.

Bibliography

Adger, W. N. "Social Capital, Collective Action, and Adaptation to Climate Change." *Economic Geography* 79, no. 4 (October 2003): 387–404. http://www.jstor.org/stable/30032945.

———. "Social and Ecological Resilience: Are They Related?" *Progress in Human Geography* 24, no. 3 (2000): 347–364. http://phg.sagepub.com/content/24/3/347.

Adger, W. N., P. M. Kelly, C. Locke, A. Winkels, and L. Q. Huy. "Migration, Remittances, Livelihood Trajectories, and Social Resilience." *Ambio* 31, no. 4 (June 2002): 358–366. http://beta.www.populationenvironmentresearch.org/papers/Vietnam_Coastal.pdf.

Ager, Alastair, and Joey Ager. *Faith, Secularism, and Humanitarian Engagement: Finding the Place of Religion in the Support of Displaced Communities*. New York: Palgrave Macmillan, 2015.

Ager, J., E. Fiddian-Qasmiyeh, and A. Ager. "Local Faith Communities and the Promotion of Resilience in Contexts of Humanitarian Crisis." *Journal of Refugee Studies* 28, no. 2 (2015): 202–221. https://doi.org/10.1093/jrs/fev001.

Ajlouny, J. "The Courage to Engage Each Other." In *Indivisible: Global Leaders on Shared Security*, edited by R. Freeman and K. Kennedy, 103–112. New York: Olive Branch Press, 2018.

Aldrich, D. P. *Building Resilience: Social Capital in Post-Disaster Recovery*. Chicago: University of Chicago Press, 2012.

Aldrich, D. P., and K. C. Crook. "Strong Civil Society as a Double-Edged Sword: Siting Trailers in Post-Katrina New Orleans." *Political Research Quarterly* 61, no. 3 (2008): 379–389. https://doi.org/10.1177/1065912907312983.

Appleby, R. S. *The Ambivalence of the Sacred: Religion, Violence, and Reconciliation*. Lanham: Rowman & Littlefield, 2000.

Ayers, Josh. "Social Capital, Resilience, and the Local Church: Ayeyarwady Delta, Myanmar." MA diss., Centre for Development & Emergency Practice (CENDEP), Oxford Brookes University, 2014.

Bahadur, Aditya V., Maggie Ibrahim, and Thomas Tanner. "The Resilience Renaissance? Unpacking of Resilience for Tackling Climate Change and Disasters." IDS Strengthening Climate Resilience Discussion Paper 1, 2010.

Baron, S., J. Field, and T. Schuller. *Social Capital: Critical Perspectives*. New York: Oxford University Press, 2002.

Barrett-Fox, Rebecca. *God Hates: Westboro Baptist Church, American Nationalism, and the Religious Right*. Lawrence: University Press of Kansas, 2016.

Bava, S., E. Coffey, K. Weingarten, and C. Becker. "Lessons in Collaboration, Four Years Post-Katrina." *Family Process* 49, no. 4 (2010): 543–558.

Bebbington, A. "Sharp Knives and Blunt Instruments: Social Capital in Development Studies." *Antipode* 34, no. 4 (2002): 800–803.

Beggs, J. J., V. A. Haines, and J. S. Hurlbert. "Situational Contingencies Surrounding the Receipt of Informal Support." *Social Forces* 75, no. 1 (1996): 201–222.

Béné, C., R. G. Wood, A. Newsham, and M. Davies. "Resilience: New Utopia or New Tyranny? Reflection about the Potentials and Limits of the Concept of Resilience in Relation to Vulnerability Reduction Programmes." *IDS Working Paper* 405 (2012): 1–61.

Benner, C., and M. Pastor. "Whither Resilience Regions? Equity, Growth, and Community." *Journal of Urban Affairs* 38, no. 1 (2016): 5–24.

Berkes, Fikret. "Understanding Uncertainty and Reducing Vulnerability: Lessons from Resilience Thinking." *Natural Hazards* 41, no. 2 (May 2007): 283–295. https://doi.org/10.1007/s11069-006-9036-7.

Betancur, J. "Gentrification and Community Fabric in Chicago." *Urban Studies* 48, no. 2 (2011): 383–406. https://doi.org/10.1177/0042098009360680.

Boan, D., B. Andrews, K. Drake, J. Polson, and H. Rosette. "Disasters, Social Justice, and the Responsibility of the Church." In *Why Oh God: Disaster, Resilience and the People of God*, edited by A. Gorospe, C. Ringma, and Hollenbeck-Wuest. Manila: Asian Theological Seminary, 2017.

Boan, D., B. Andrews, K. Sanders, D. Martinson, E. Loewer, and J. Aten. "A Qualitative Study of an Indigenous Faith-Based Distributive Justice Program in Kakuma Refugee Camp in Kenya." *Christian Journal for Global Health* [S.l.] 5, no. 2 (2018): 3–20. https://doi.org/10.15566/cjgh.v5i2.215.

Boan, D., J. Aten, S. Greener, and R. Gailey. "The Well Prepared International Development Worker." *Missiology* 44 (2016): 430–447.

Bourdieu, Pierre. "Forms of Capital." In *Handbook of Theory and Research for the Sociology of Education,* edited by J. Richardson, 241–260. Westport: Greenwood Press, 1986.

Box, G., W. Hunter, and S. Hunter. *Statistics for Experimenters: Design, Innovation, and Discovery.* 2nd ed. Hoboken, NJ: John Wiley & Sons, 2005.

Brown, R. K., and R. E. Brown. "Faith and Works: Church-Based Social Capital Resources and African American Political Activism." *Social Forces* 82, no. 2 (December 2003): 617–641. https://www.jstor.org/stable/3598204.

Bruyn, S. "The Moral Economy." *Review of Social Economy* 57, no. 1 (1999): 25–46.

Burchardt, Marian. "Faith-Based Humanitarianism: Organizational Change and Everyday Meanings in South Africa." *Sociology of Religion* 74, no. 1 (2013): 30–55.

Burgess, R. "African Pentecostal Spirituality and Civic Engagement: The Case of the Redeemed Christian Church of God in Britain." *Journal of Beliefs & Values* 30, no. 3 (December 2009): 255–273.

Calhoun, Craig, "Civil Society and the Public Sphere." In *The Oxford Handbook of Civil Society*, edited by Michael Edwards, 311–323. New York: Oxford University Press, 2011.

Carron, A. V., and L. R. Brawley. "Cohesion: Conceptual and Measurement Issues." *Small Group Research* 31, no. 1 (2000): 89–106.

Carron, A. V., L. R. Brawley, and W. N. Widmeyer. "The Measurement of Cohesion in Sports Teams: The Group Environment Questionnaire." *Canadian Journal of Sport Science* 14, no. 1 (1988): 55–59.

Chambers, S., and J. Kopstein. "Bad Civil Society." *Political Theory* 29, no. 6 (2001): 837–865.

Cheema, A. R., R. Scheyvens, B. Glavovic, and M. Imran. "Unnoticed but Important: Revealing the Hidden Contribution of Community-Based Religious Institution of the Mosque in Disasters." *Natural Hazards* 71, no. 3 (April 2014): 2207–2229.

Clarke, M. "Good Works and God's Work: A Case Study of Churches and Community Development in Vanuatu." *Asia Pacific Viewpoint* 54, no. 3 (2013): 340–351.

Coleman, J. S. "Social Capital in the Creation of Human Capital." *American Journal of Sociology* 94 (1988): S95–S120. http://www.jstor.org/stable/2780243.

Colson, Charles, and Nancy Pearcey. *How Now Shall We Live?* Carol Stream, IL: Tyndale House, 2004.

Cox, Robin, and Karen-Marie Perry. "Like a Fish Out of Water: Reconsidering Disaster Recovery and the Role of Place and Social Capital in Community Disaster Resilience." *American Journal of Community Psychology* 48 (2011): 395–411. https://doi.org/10.1007/s10464-011-9427-0.

Cutter, S., B. Boruff, and W. Shirley. "Social Vulnerability to Environmental Hazards." *Social Science Quarterly* 84, no. 2 (June 2003): 242–261.

Cutter, S., and C. Emrich. "Moral Hazard, Social Catastrophe: The Changing Face of Vulnerability along the Hurricane Coasts." *The ANNALS of the American Academy of Political and Social Science* 604 (2006): 102.

Cutter, S. L., L. Barnes, M. Berry, C. Burton, E. Evans, E. Tate, and J. Webb. "A Place-Based Model for Understanding Community Resilience to Natural Disasters." *Global Environmental Change* 18, no. 4 (October 2008): 598–606. https://doi.org/10.1016/j.gloenvcha.2008.07.013.

Deneulin, Séverine, and Masooda Bano. *Religion in Development: Rewriting the Secular Script.* London: Zed Books, 2009.

Djalante, R., C. Holley, F. Thomalla, and M. Carnegie. "Pathways for Adaptive and Integrated Disaster Resilience." *Natural Hazards* 69, no. 3 (2013): 2105–2135.

Djupe, P. A., A. E. Sokhey, and C. P. Gilbert. "Present but Not Accounted For? Gender Differences in Civic Resource Acquisition." *American Journal of Political Science* 51, no. 4 (October 2007): 906–920. http://www.jstor.org/stable/4620107.

Doehring, Carrie. "Resilience as the Relational Ability to Spiritually Integrate Moral Stress." *Pastoral Psychology* 64, no. 5 (October 2015): 635–649.

Doehring, C., and K. Arora. "Spiritually-Integrated Financial Resilience: Helping Seminary Students Respond to Financial Stress." *Theological Education* 51, no. 1 (2017): 17–28.

Dordick, G. *Something Left to Lose: Personal Relations and Survival among New York's Homeless*. Philadelphia: Temple University Press, 1997.

Dynes, R. R., and E. L. Quarantelli. "A Brief Note on Disaster Restoration, Reconstruction and Recovery: A Comparative Note Using Post Earthquake Observations." Preliminary Paper #359. Newark: University of Delaware Disaster Research Center, 2008. http://udspace.udel.edu/handle/19716/3058.

Elliott, James R., and Junia Howell. "Beyond Disasters: A Longitudinal Analysis of Natural Hazards' Unequal Impacts on Residential Instability." *Social Forces* 95, no. 3 (2017): 1181–1207.

Fiddian-Qasmiyeh, Elena, and Alastair Ager. "Local Faith Communities and the Promotion of Resilience in Humanitarian Situations." *University of Oxford Refugee Studies Centre Working Paper Series No. 90* (2013): 1–62.

Folke, Carl. "Resilience: The Emergence of a Perspective for Social–Ecological Systems Analyses." *Global Environmental Change* 16, no. 3 (August 2006): 253–267. https://doi.org/10.1016/j.gloenvcha.2006.04.002.

Francis, D. "The Things That Make for Peace." In *Indivisible: Global Leaders on Shared Security*, edited by R. Freeman and K. Kennedy, 165–174. New York: Olive Branch Press, 2018.

Freeman, R. and K. Kennedy. *Indivisible: Global Leaders on Shared Security*. New York: Olive Branch Press, 2018.

Fritz, J., A. M. de Graaff, H. Caisley, A. L. van Harmelen, and P. O. Wilkinson. "A Systematic Review of Amenable Resilience Factors That Moderate and/or Mediate the Relationship between Childhood Adversity and Mental Health in Young People." *Frontiers in Psychiatry* 9 (2018): 230. https://www.ncbi.nlm.nih.gov/pubmed/29971021.

Fukuyama, Francis. *Trust: The Social Virtues and The Creation of Prosperity*. New York: Free Press, 1995.

Granovetter, M. S. "The Strength of Weak Ties." *American Journal of Sociology* 78, no. 6 (1973): 1360–1380.

Gill, Timothy. *Making Things Worse*. Utrecht: Dalit Network Netherlands (DNN), 2007.

Gittell, Ross, and Avis Vidal. *Community Organizing: Building Social Capital as a Development Strategy*. Washington, DC: SAGE Publications, 1998.

Haynes, Jeffrey. *Religion and Development: Conflict or Cooperation?* Houndmills: Palgrave Macmillan, 2007.

Hobfoll, S. E., and R. S. Lilly. "Resource Conservation as a Strategy for Community Psychology." *Journal of Community Psychology* 21, no. 2 (1993): 128–148. https://psycnet.apa.org/record/1993-37500-001.

Holling, C. S. "Resilience and Stability of Ecological Systems." *Annual Review of Ecology and Systematics* 4 (1973): 1–23.

Holton, M. J. "'Our Hope Comes from God': Faith Narratives and Resilience in Southern Sudan." *Journal of Pastoral Theology* 20 (2010): 67–84.

Hou, W. K., L. Francisco, C. Hougen, B. Hall, and S. Hobfoll. "Measuring Everyday Processes and Mechanisms of Stress Resilience: Development and Initial Validation of the Sustainability of Living Inventory (SOLI)." *Psychological Assessment* 31 (2019): 715–729. https://doi.org/10.1037/pas0000692.

Howell, Junia, and James R. Elliott. "As Disaster Costs Rise, So Does Inequality." *Socius: Sociological Research for a Dynamic World* 4 (2018). https://doi.org/10.1177/2378023118816795.

IFRC. "Characteristics of a Safe and Resilient Community: Community Based Disaster Risk Reduction Study." *ARUP International Development* (September 2011). https://resourcecentre.savethechildren.net/node/6541/pdf/6541.pdf.

———. "The Road to Resilience: Bridging Relief and Development for a More Sustainable Future." *IFRC Discussion Paper on Resilience* (2012). https://resourcecentre.savethechildren.net/node/6299/pdf/6299.pdf.

Imperiale, A. J., and F. Vanclay. "Experiencing Local Community Resilience: Learning from Post-Disaster Communities." *Journal of Rural Studies* 47 (2016): 204–219. https://doi.org/10.1016/j.jrurstud.2016.08.002.

Joint Learning Initiative on Faith & Local Communities (JLIF&LC). "Evidence for Religious Groups' Contributions to Humanitarian Response." 2016. https://jliflc.com/wp-content/uploads/2016/05/201605_Key-Messages_04-ONLINE.pdf.

Kahn, W. A., M. A. Barton, C. M. Fisher, E. D. Heaphy, E. M. Reid, and E. D. Rouse. "The Geography of Strain: Organizational Resilience as a Function of Intergroup Relations." *Academy of Management Review* 43, no. 3 (2018): 509–529. https://doi.org/10.5465/amr.2016.0004.

Kame, G., and R. S. Tshaka. "Morality and Spirituality: The Missing Link for Economic Development in the 21st Century." *HTS Teologiese Studies/Theological Studies* 71, no. 3 (2015): 1–6. https://doi.org/10.4102/hts.v71i3.2818.

King Jr., Martin Luther. *Letter from Birmingham Jail*. Westminster: Penguin Random House, 1968.

Kirmayer, L., M. Sehdev, R. Whitley, S. Dandeneau, and C. Isaac. "Community Resilience: Models, Metaphors and Measures." *Journal of Aboriginal Health* 5, no. 1 (2013): 62–117.

Kraft, K., and S. Manar. "Hope for the Middle East: The Impact and Significance of the Christian Presence in Syria and Iraq: Past, Present and Future." Edited by Stephen Rand. Open Doors, Served, University of East London's Centre for Social Justice and Change, and Middle East Concern, 2016. http://www.opendoorsuk.org/campaign/documents/H4ME-report.pdf.

Laws, E., and H. Marquette. "Thinking and Working Politically: Reviewing the Evidence on the Integration of Politics into Development Practice over the Past Decade." *Thinking and Working Politically (TWP) Community of Practice*. London: Overseas Development Institute (ODI) and University of Birmingham, 2018.

Lerner, M., and S. Clayton. *Justice and Self-Interest: Two Fundamental Motives*. Cambridge: Cambridge University Press, 2011.

Lidskog, R. "Invented Communities and Social Vulnerability: The Local Post-Disaster Dynamics of Extreme Environmental Events." *Sustainability* 10 (2018): 1–19. https://doi.org/10.3390/su10124457.

Lin, N. "A Network Theory of Social Capital." In *The Handbook of Social Capital*, edited by Dario Castiglione, Jan W. van Deth, and Guglielmo Wolleb, 50–69. Oxford: Oxford University Press, 2008.

Mansour, K. "(In)Securing Each Other." In *Indivisible: Global Leaders on Shared Security*, edited by R. Freeman and K. Kennedy, 113–120. New York: Olive Branch Press, 2018.

Mayer, B., K. Running, and K. Bergstrand. "Compensation and Community Corrosion: Perceived Inequalities, Social Comparisons, and Competition Following the Deepwater Horizon Oil Spill." *Sociological Forum* 30, no. 2 (2015): 369–390. https://doi.org/10.1111/socf.12167.

Mayunga, J. S. "Understanding and Applying the Concept of Community Disaster Resilience: A Capital-Based Approach." *Summer Academy for Social Vulnerability and Resilience Building* (January 2007): 1–16.

Menocal, A. R., M. Cassidy, S. Swift, D. Jacobstein, C. Rothblum, and I. Tservil. *Thinking and Working Politically through Applied Political Economy Analysis: A Guide for Practitioners.* Washington, DC: USAID DCHA Bureau Center of Excellence on Democracy, Human Rights and Governance, 2018. Available at: https://usaidlearninglab.org/sites/default/files/resource/files/pea_guide_final.pdf.

Messer, Chris M., Thomas E. Shriver, and Dennis Kennedy. "Environmental Hazards and Community Dissension in Rural Oklahoma." *Sociological Spectrum* 30, no. 2 (2010): 159–183. https://doi.org/10.1080/02732170903496034.

Miller, D. S. "Visualizing the Corrosive Community: Looting in the Aftermath of Hurricane Katrina." *Space and Culture* 9, no. 1 (2006): 71–73. https://doi.org/10.1177/1206331205283762.

Nakagawa, Y., and R. Shaw. "Social Capital: A Missing Link to Disaster Recovery." *International Journal of Mass Emergencies and Disasters* 22, no. 1 (2004): 5–34.

Narayan, D., R. Chambers, M. K. Shah, and P. Petesch. *Voices of the Poor: Crying Out for Change.* Oxford: Oxford University Press for the World Bank, 2000.

Newton, Kenneth. "Social Capital and Democracy." *American Behavioral Scientist* 40 (1997): 575–586.

Norris, F. H., S. P. Stevens, B. Pfefferbaum, K. F. Wyche, and R. L. Pfefferbaum. "Community Resilience as a Metaphor, Theory, Set of Capacities, and Strategy for Disaster Readiness." *American Journal of Community Psychology* 41, no. 1–2 (2008): 127–150.

Nyamutera, J. "Truth and Reconciliation." Paper presented at the Micah Global Triennial meeting, Lima, Peru, September 2015.

Offutt, S., F. D. Bronkema, K. Vaillancourt Murphy, R. Davis, and G. Okesson. *Advocating Justice: An Evangelical Vision for Transforming Systems and Structures.* Grand Rapids: Baker Academic, 2016.

Ögtem-Young, Ö. "Faith Resilience: Everyday Experiences." *Societies* 8, no. 1 (2018): 10. https://doi.org/10.3390/soc8010010.

Padilla, R. "Introduction: An Ecclesiology of Integral Mission." In *The Local Church, Agent of Transformation*, edited by T. Yamamori and R. Padilla. Buenos Aires: Kairos, 2004.

Paton, D., R. Bajek, N. Okada, and D. McIvor. "Predicting Community Earthquake Preparedness: A Cross-Cultural Comparison of Japan and New Zealand." *Natural Hazards* 54 (2010): 765–781. https://doi.org/10.1007/s11069-010-9500-2.

Pelling, M. *The Vulnerability of Cities: Natural Disasters and Social Resilience*. London: Routledge, 2003.

Portes, A., and J. Sensenbrenner. "Embeddedness and Immigration: Notes on the Social Determinants of Economic Action." *American Journal of Sociology* 98, no. 6 (May 1993): 1320–1350. http://www.jstor.org/stable/2781823.

Powelson, J. *The Moral Economy*. Ann Arbor: University of Michigan Press, 1998.

Putnam, R. D. *Bowling Alone: The Collapse and Revival of American Community*. New York: Simon & Schuster, 2000.

———. *Making Democracy Work: Civic Traditions in Modern Italy*. Princeton: Princeton University Press, 1993.

Reich, G., and P. Dos Santos. "The Rise (and Frequent Fall) of Evangelical Politicians: Organization, Theology, and Church Politics." *Latin American Politics and Society* 55, no. 4 (Dec 2013): 1–22.

Rich, G., S. Sirikantraporn, and W. Jean-Charles. "The Concept of Posttraumatic Growth in an Adult Sample from Port-au-Prince, Haiti." In *Human Strengths and Resilience*, edited by Grant J. Rich and Skultip Sirikantraporn, 21–38. London: Lexington Books, 2018.

Samuel, C. B. "Doing Justice God's Way." Presentation to 2018 Micah Triennial, Philippines, 2018.

Sen, Amartya. *Development as Freedom*. New York: Anchor Books, 1999.

Shepherd, A., L. Scott, C. Mariotti, F. Kessy, R. Gaiha, L. da Corta, K. Hanifnia, N. Kaicker, A. Lenhardt, C. Lwanga-Ntale, B. Sen, B. Sijapati, T. Strawson, G. Thapa, H. Underhill, and L. Wild. *The Chronic Poverty Report 2014–2015: The Road to Zero Extreme Poverty*. London: Chronic Poverty Advisory Network (CPAN) and Overseas Development Institute (ODI), 2014. https://www.odi.org/sites/odi.org.uk/files/odi-assets/publications-opinion-files/8834.pdf.

Sherrieb, K., F. H. Norris, and D. Galea. "Measuring Capacities for Community Resilience." *Social Indicators Research* 99, no. 2 (2010): 227–247.

Smiley, Kevin T., Junia Howell, and James R. Elliott. "Disasters, Local Organizations and Poverty in the USA, 1998 to 2015." *Population and Environment* 40, no. 2 (2018): 115–135. https://doi.org/10.1007/s11111-018-0304-8.

Smith, L. C., and T. R. Frankenberger. "Does Resilience Capacity Reduce the Negative Impact of Shocks on Household Food Security? Evidence from the 2014 Floods in Northern Bangladesh." *World Development* 102 (2018): 358–376. https://doi.org.nnu.idm.oclc.org/10.1016/j.worlddev.2017.07.003.

Snyder, J., D. Boan, J. Aten, W. Davis, and L. Van Grinsven. "Resource Loss and Stress Outcomes Following Armed Conflict in Africa: Examining Conservation of Resources Theory in the Eastern Democratic Republic of the Congo." *Journal of Traumatic Stress* (forthcoming).

Stearns, Richard. *The Hole in Our Gospel.* Nashville: Thomas Nelson, 2014.

Stephan, M. "People Power as Shared Security." In *Indivisible: Global Leaders on Shared Security,* edited by R. Freeman and K. Kennedy, 203–210. New York: Olive Branch Press, 2018.

Szreter, S. "The State of Social Capital: Bringing Back in Power, Politics, and History." *Theory and Society* 31, no. 5 (October 2002): 573–621.

Szreter, S., and M. Woolcock. "Health by Association? Social Capital, Social Theory and the Political Economy of Public Health." *International Journal of Epidemiology* 33, no. 4 (August 2004): 650–667.

Talò, C. "Community-Based Determinants of Community Engagement: A Meta-Analysis Research." *Social Indicators Research* 140, no. 2 (2018): 571–596. https://doi.org/10.1007/s11205-017-1778-y.

Tatsuki, S., and H. Hayashi. "Seven Critical Element Model of Life Recovery: General Linear Model Analyses of the 2001 Kobe Panel Survey Data." In *Research Center for Disaster Reduction Systems. 2nd Workshop for Comparative Study on Urban Earthquake Disaster Management. Kobe, Japan, 14–15 February 2002.* Kobe: Disaster Prevention Research Institute, Kyoto University, 2002. https://pdfs.semanticscholar.org/b5f9/d62b0364f30db564e9eb4c1dada4e5cbc83d.pdf?_ga=2.211185814.28303261.1582538283-2084511550.1544117297.

Tierney, Kathleen. *The Social Roots of Risk.* Stanford: Stanford University Press, 2014.

Todd, Scott C. *Fast Living: How the Church Will End Extreme Poverty.* Colorado Springs: Compassion International, 2011.

Twigg, J. *Characteristics of a Disaster-Resilient Community.* London: UCL Hazard Research Centre, 2009.

Ungar, M. "The Social Ecology of Resilience: Addressing Contextual and Cultural Ambiguity of a Nascent Construct." *American Journal of Orthopsychiatry* 81, no. 1 (January 2011): 1–17.

———. *The Social Ecology of Resilience: A Handbook of Theory and Practice.* New York: Springer, 2012.

Ungar, M., M. Ghazinour, and J. Richter. "Annual Research Review: What Is Resilience within the Social Ecology of Human Development?" *Journal of Child Psychology and Psychiatry* 54, no. 4 (2013): 348–366. https://doi.org/10.1111/jcpp.12025.

Van Eymeren, A. "Creating Shalom in the City: A Roadmap for Human Flourishing." In *Urban Shalom and the Cities We Need,* edited by A. Van Eymeren, A. Barker, B. McCabe and C. Elisara, 11–28. Birmingham, UK: Urban Shalom Publishing, 2017.

Weick, K. "Faith, Evidence, and Action: Better Guesses in an Unknowable World." *Organization Studies* 27, no. 11 (2006): 1–14.

Weijer, Frauke. "Resilience: A Trojan Horse for a New Way of Thinking?" *ECDPM Discussion Paper 139* (2013): 1–26.

Wilkinson, Olivia. "'Faith Can Come In, but Not Religion': Secularity and Its Effects on the Disaster Response to Typhoon Haiyan." *Disasters* 42, no. 3 (October 24, 2017): 459–474. https://doi.org/10.1111/disa.12258.

Wetterberg, A. "Crisis, Social Ties, and Household Welfare: Testing Social Capital Theory with Evidence from Indonesia." Washington, DC: World Bank Group, 2004. http://documents.worldbank.org/curated/en/807921468043505094/pdf/3 42230IND0Social0capital01PUBLIC1.pdf.

Wilson-Hartgrove, Jonathan. *Reconstructing the Gospel: Finding Freedom from Slaveholder Religion*. Grand Rapids: IVP Books, 2018.

Woolcock, M. "Social Capital and Economic Development: Toward a Theoretical Synthesis and Policy Framework." *Theory and Society* 27, no. 2 (1998): 151–208.

———. "Social Capital in Theory and Practice: Reducing Poverty by Building Partnerships between States, Markets and Civil Society." In *United Nations Educational, Scientific and Cultural Organization (UNESCO), Social Capital Formation in Poverty Reduction: Which Role for the Civil Society Organizations and the State? (Symposium)*. Geneva, Switzerland, 2000, 18–39.

World Evangelical Alliance. "A Call to Commitment and Partnership: A World Evangelical Alliance Brief on the Evangelical Community and Humanitarian Development." New York: World Evangelical Alliance, 2015.

Wulff, K., D. Donato, and N. Lurie. "What Is Health Resilience and How Can We Build It?" *Annual Review of Public Health* 36 (2015): 361–374. https://doi.org/10.1146/annurev-publhealth-031914-122829.

Index

Micah's Vision

Communities living life in all its fullness, free from poverty, injustice and conflict.

Micah's Mission

Rooted in the Gospel we become agents of change in our communities by being:

- **Catalysts** for transforming mission by promoting and living out **integral mission**
- A **movement** that advocates for poverty reduction, justice, equality, reconciliation and safety and wellbeing for all
- A **network** providing a platform for shared learning, collective reflection and action, inspiration and mobilisation of the Church, and the demonstration of Integral Mission.

Why Does Micah Exist?

Micah exists to be a catalyst, a movement and a network for **transforming mission**, with a special focus on enabling a united response to reducing poverty, addressing injustice and enabling reconciliation and conflict resolution.

We believe that Jesus came to give life in all its fullness (John 10:10). We believe that God has called out his church (*ecclesia*) to be his body, his representatives, his servants, and to demonstrate the new Kingdom in word and deed. We call this **integral mission**.

To learn more about Micah Global see: www.micahglobal.org
Find us on Facebook: www.facebook.com/MicahNetwork
Follow us on Twitter: @MicahGlobal
Enjoy our Instagram: www.instagram.com/micahglobal

Micah Global

PO Box 381, Carlisle, CA1 9FE, United Kingdom
Email: info@micahglobal.org
Phone: +44 1228 231 073

Langham Literature and its imprints are a ministry of Langham Partnership.

Langham Partnership is a global fellowship working in pursuit of the vision God entrusted to its founder John Stott –

> *to facilitate the growth of the church in maturity and Christ-likeness through raising the standards of biblical preaching and teaching.*

Our vision is to see churches in the Majority World equipped for mission and growing to maturity in Christ through the ministry of pastors and leaders who believe, teach and live by the Word of God.

Our mission is to strengthen the ministry of the Word of God through:
- nurturing national movements for biblical preaching
- fostering the creation and distribution of evangelical literature
- enhancing evangelical theological education

especially in countries where churches are under-resourced.

Our ministry

Langham Preaching partners with national leaders to nurture indigenous biblical preaching movements for pastors and lay preachers all around the world. With the support of a team of trainers from many countries, a multi-level programme of seminars provides practical training, and is followed by a programme for training local facilitators. Local preachers' groups and national and regional networks ensure continuity and ongoing development, seeking to build vigorous movements committed to Bible exposition.

Langham Literature provides Majority World preachers, scholars and seminary libraries with evangelical books and electronic resources through publishing and distribution, grants and discounts. The programme also fosters the creation of indigenous evangelical books in many languages, through writer's grants, strengthening local evangelical publishing houses, and investment in major regional literature projects, such as one-volume Bible commentaries like *The Africa Bible Commentary* and *The South Asia Bible Commentary*.

Langham Scholars provides financial support for evangelical doctoral students from the Majority World so that, when they return home, they may train pastors and other Christian leaders with sound, biblical and theological teaching. This programme equips those who equip others. Langham Scholars also works in partnership with Majority World seminaries in strengthening evangelical theological education. A growing number of Langham Scholars study in high quality doctoral programmes in the Majority World itself. As well as teaching the next generation of pastors, graduated Langham Scholars exercise significant influence through their writing and leadership.

To learn more about Langham Partnership and the work we do visit **langham.org**

Lightning Source UK Ltd.
Milton Keynes UK
UKHW021828130320
360317UK00005B/115